NARROW GAUGE
STEAM LOCOMOTIVES

Brian Solomon

MBI Publishing Company

DEDICATION

To Robert A. Buck—
who helped foster my interest in railways
and who introduced me to narrow gauge railroading some years ago.

First published in 1999 by MBI Publishing Company, 729 Prospect Avenue, PO Box 1, Osceola, WI 54020-0001 USA

MBI Publishing Company books are also available at discounts in bulk quantity for industrial or sales-promotional use. For details write to Special Sales Manager at Motorbooks International Wholesalers & Distributors, 729 Prospect Avenue, Osceola, WI 54020-0001 USA.

Library of Congress Cataloging-in-Publication Data Available

ISBN 0-7603-0543-9

On the front cover: Durango & Silverton K-36 480 leads a southbound train along a narrow shelf above Shalona Lake, a short distance from Rockwood, Colorado. *Brian Solomon*

On the frontispiece: The narrow gauge was simply and cheaply built, typically with dirt ballast and minimal roadbed. In places, the tracks are visible only to the careful observer. The rails of the Big Horn Wye catch the glint of the rising summer sun. *Brian Solomon*

On the title page: Cumbres & Toltec K36 number 487, a 2-8-2 Mikado at Chama, New Mexico. *Brian Solomon*

On the back cover: Cumbres & Toltec K36-class locomotives at Chama, New Mexico. *Brian Solomon*

Edited by Kris Palmer
Designed by Rebecca Allen

Printed in Hong Kong

CONTENTS

ACKNOWLEDGMENTS

I'm indebted to many individuals and extremely grateful to them for their assistance with this book. John Gruber, editor of *Vintage Rails,* has been especially helpful; in addition to writing the sidebar on narrow gauge photography, he provided a number of images used in this book and lent me source materials that proved very useful in researching the text. Tom S. Hoover has explored various narrow gauge railways with me over the years, and even tolerated an extra morning on the Durango & Silverton some years ago when he had a thousand-mile drive before him. Tom's father, Tom A. Hoover, a lifelong East Broad Top observer, has been a gracious host on many occasions and has accompanied me on several EBT adventures, including hiking trips to locate EBT's abandoned tunnels and disused facilities. Mel Patrick helped with proofreading, critical photographic judgment, and the use of his house while I was on extended trips in Colorado; he also pointed out remains of the Rio Grande narrow gauge right-of-way in the Utah Desert. Ed Beaudette is a long-time friend who helped in many ways and graciously showed me numerous photo locations on Cumbres Pass. Sean Kelly of Tralee, Co., Kerry, Ireland, brought me to visit the Tralee & Dingle narrow gauge. Keith Thomasson of Blaenau Ffestiniog, Wales, showed me Welsh 2-foot gauge lines. My father, Richard J. Solomon, lent me the use of his extensive book collection and assisted in proofreading. Thanks to the contributing photographers, including Mike Gardner, Brian Jennison, Joe McMillan, Hal Miller, and Jim Speaker.

The Cumbres-Toltec blowing steam at Tanglefoot curve.

Chapter 1

History of Narrow Gauge Railways

Compelling, attractive, romantic, and historic, the remaining segments of the once vast American narrow gauge railway system provide a wonderful way to relax and interact with historical technology amidst inspiring scenery. It's no surprise that every year hundreds of thousands of people ride extant narrow gauge lines. Interest in these routes has perpetuated their existence long after remote narrow gauge railways ceased being a competitive and profitable method of transportation.

The United States was among the earliest nations to adopt the narrow gauge and for many years was the foremost operator, by mileage, of narrow gauge railways. Agile, narrow gauge trains climbed mountains and reached mines and other resources more cheaply and easily than standard lines, opening up new opportunities in remote areas. Carrying silver, coal, bricks, oil, livestock, passengers, and a broad array of other goods and supplies, these diminutive trains linked people, places, and products that had once been isolated. Though depletion of the mines and the rise of highway transport would finally bring an end to the narrow gauge era, this fascinating period lives on in a few carefully preserved lines.

Today, the former Denver & Rio Grande narrow gauge lines in southwestern Colorado and northern New Mexico, and the East Broad Top in Pennsylvania, are the most prominent examples of traditional 3-foot gauge railway—the standard for American narrow gauge, common-carrier lines. While not the only remaining narrow gauge lines, these railways well deserve the attention they are given.

The Rio Grande and East Broad Top are notable for several reasons. Both were pioneering American narrow gauge lines that set precedent for further narrow gauge construction. They were both integrated with standard gauge railway systems, permitting interchange of freight and passenger traffic. Both lines relied heavily on mineral traffic, but also carried passengers throughout most of their existence. These lines continued to invest and maintain narrow gauge standards, and to upgrade and modernize their motive power and equipment fleets, long after most other American narrow gauge railways had folded or converted to standard gauge. Fortunately, they survived long enough to be recognized and preserved.

The Cumbres & Toltec and East Broad Top are two of the best-preserved railways in the United States. Although these railways have been adapted as tourist haulers, they use equipment and facilities that are historically correct. Where other tourist railways and railway museums in the United States operate and display a potpourri

The Durango & Silverton Narrow Gauge is one of the most popular scenic railways in the United States. In the summer, as many as four trains a day run between Durango and Silverton, Colorado. On an August 1991 morning a K-28 Mikado passes through Durango on its way north.

Previous pages
Perhaps the most spectacular American narrow gauge scene is the grueling 4 percent grade of the former Denver & Rio Grande from Chama, New Mexico, to the summit of Cumbres Pass, Colorado. Two Cumbres & Toltec narrow gauge Mikados work this steep, sinuous, scenic route in September 1998.

Narrow gauge was once prevalent all over the United States, and many narrow gauge railways were later converted to standard gauge. In the 1920s, Southern Pacific purchased the 3-foot gauge Nevada-California-Oregon line and incorporated it in its standard gauge Modoc Line. The Modoc's winding tracks and spartan railroad bed reveal its narrow gauge past. In May 1994, a Southern Pacific freight climbs toward Indian Camp, California.

of railway equipment, representing a variety of different periods, equipment styles and geographical areas, these narrow gauge lines are reasonably authentic. With minor exceptions made for some passenger cars and work equipment, these narrow gauge railways are operated with appropriate equipment.

The steam locomotives that regularly operate on these lines today are the very same locomotives that hauled freight and passenger traffic near the turn of the century. Although both the C&T and EBT own some "off line" equipment and locomotives for maintenance purposes, they don't regularly operate a collection of locomotives that have no historical precedent on the line.

The traditional structures and pristine character of the lines' facilities at Chama, New Mexico, and Orbisonia, Pennsylvania, are a treat for enthusiasts, accurately reflecting railway operations of an earlier era. Their appearance today is much as it was more than 50 years ago. Dedication to historical authenticity distinguishes these two railways from many American tourist railways and museums that have sacrificed historical authenticity for public convenience. True to their time, the C&T and EBT lines lack asphalt sidewalks, phony "old-time" signs and many contemporary amenities that serve convenience rather than historical interpretation.

The East Broad Top narrow gauge in Pennsylvania is one of the best-preserved and most uncluttered historical railways in the United States. It's a virtual time capsule of railway history: here, an 80-year-old Baldwin Mikado climbs a short grade north of Orbisonia, Pennsylvania, on a clear morning in September 1996—40 years after the line was sold for scrap.

The Cumbres & Toltec, Durango & Silverton, and East Broad Top lines are isolated narrow gauge fragments of once-larger networks. At the time they were built, narrow gauge railways were promoted worldwide as an economical solution for areas with light traffic and difficult terrain. While the Rio Grande and East Broad Top narrow gauge lines are among the most prominent, other less-known lines—some preserved for tourism and historical purposes, others operating as transportation systems—still exist around the world.

Noteworthy Domestic Narrow Gauge Lines

In their heyday, narrow gauge lines operated in most of the 50 states. Maine once boasted a substantial network of 2-foot gauge railways, some of which survived into the 1940s. Several of Maine's 2-foot gauge locomotives are preserved. Many of these operated for years on the tourist-oriented Edaville line in South Carver, Massachusetts, but most have since returned to Maine where preservation efforts are underway.

California also hosted a variety of narrow gauge railways, and a few survived into the early 1960s. Southern Pacific's "Slim Princess," the Carson & Colorado, was a 3-foot gauge line operating on the eastern side of the Sierra Nevada. It connected with Southern Pacific's standard gauge on each end. Until the 1930s, this spectacular line operated over Montgomery Pass, but was truncated during the Great Depression. It survived as a steam-powered railway longer than SP's standard gauge lines, and was one of the few American narrow gauge common carriers to convert to diesel power before finally being abandoned. Several of Southern Pacific's 3-foot gauge 2-6-0's (locomotives with 2 leading wheels, 6 drive wheels, and no trailing wheels—see Chapter 5), which served the line, are preserved. One is displayed at Independence, California—one of several remote villages served by the narrow gauge; another is at the narrow gauge railroad museum in Laws, California.

In many countries narrow gauge remains common. Most of Japan's extensive railway network uses meter-gauge tracks (about 3 1/3 inches wider than 3-foot gauge). A meter-gauge electric streamliner approaches Osaka station on April 25, 1996.

Narrow gauge tracks at Boston Lodge, Wales: the 2-foot gauge, slate-hauling Festiniog Railway was the prototype for William Jackson Palmer's Denver & Rio Grande narrow gauge in Colorado. Today the Festiniog survives as a popular tourist attraction.

North Wales is famous for its 2-foot gauge railways. In addition to the pioneering Festiniog, numerous other small railways attract railway enthusiasts from around the world. A 2-foot gauge articulated Garrett-type locomotive built for service in South Africa now serves the Welsh Highland Railway at Caernarvon.

The White Pass & Yukon was a 111-mile-long, 3-foot gauge line built from Skagway, Alaska, over White Pass, to British Columbia, ultimately reaching Whitehorse, Yukon Territory in 1900. The White Pass & Yukon survived longer than nearly all other American narrow gauge lines. It was one of just a few to convert from steam to diesel operation, and continued to haul freight until 1982 when the railroad was shut down. Since that time the southern end of the railroad has been reopened as a tourist line.

The demise of a narrow gauge line did not necessarily mean the end of rail service. Around the United States many narrow gauge railways were converted to standard gauge routes, and after 1886 narrow gauge conversions to standard gauge exceeded new narrow gauge construction. Some railways, such as Denver & Rio Grande, rebuilt some narrow gauge lines to standard gauge, including lines used as their mainlines, while simultaneously relocating and straightening the railroad right-of-way.

Narrow gauge railways were occasionally acquired by standard gauge railways specifically for their right-of-way. Segments of the old Nevada-California-Oregon 3-foot gauge, which crossed the desert between Reno, Nevada, and Lakeview, Oregon, by way of Alturas, California, were acquired for standard gauge adaptation by the Western Pacific and by Southern Pacific. Much of the old N-C-O line between Wendel and Alturas was used by the SP for its Alturas cutoff, also known as the Modoc line, and except for a line relocation near Crest, California, the old narrow gauge right-of-way survived as a mainline until the mid-1990s—albeit one of lightest-traveled mainlines in the western United States. (Watching one of SP's infrequent freight trains, often more than a mile long, traverse this meandering sinuous line across the desert floor was testimony to the primitive engineering of old narrow gauge.)

Today, the old Modoc line, now owned by Union Pacific, is largely out of service, but the rails remain. Farther south, another portion of the

N-C-O, now also part of Union Pacific, remains a vital transportation link. This segment was part of George Gould's Western Pacific mainline—a line funded in part from profits from another Gould property, the Denver & Rio Grande.

Narrow Gauge Around the World

The narrow gauge building frenzy that inspired the lines in the United States was part of a worldwide interest in narrow gauge lines. While these lines have long been superseded by other modes of transportation in the United States, narrow gauge survives as vital transportation in many other parts of the world. In addition, there are numerous historical narrow gauge lines, and a number of interesting narrow gauge museums.

Some nations chose narrow gauge as their "standard" gauge. The extensive railway network in Japan is meter-gauge, although its famous Shinkansen high-speed trains (often called "bullet trains" by Westerners) use the British and American standard gauge—4-feet, 8-1/2-inches. Narrow gauge lines are also used in other nations where wider gauges prevail. There are many extant narrow gauge railways in daily service throughout Europe. In Stockholm, Sweden, a network of electrified 3-foot gauge railway lines survives as a suburban commuter system despite a predominance of standard gauge railways. Switzerland and Austria boast some of the most spectacular mountain narrow gauge lines in the world. In Africa, Asia, and South America, narrow gauge lines are also common.

Wales, the birthplace of the narrow gauge movement, is famous for numerous steam-powered narrow gauge tourist lines. The pioneering Festiniog 2-foot gauge has been restored for tourist service and operates most of the year between its namesake at Blaenau Ffestiniog and Porthamadog. Its trains make connections with standard gauge trains at Blaenau Ffestiniog and

Part of the original narrow gauge line over Tennessee Pass to Red Cliff, Colorado, was incorporated into Rio Grande's standard gauge mainline from Denver to Ogden. This line remained in heavy service until 1997, when it was finally closed in favor of other routes. In September 1996, a coal train negotiates the confines of the Eagle River Canyon near Red Cliff.

Minffordd, allowing rail passengers to use the narrow gauge line as part of their journey.

Western Ireland also once boasted a significant narrow gauge network, providing feeders in lightly populated areas with difficult terrain. Like American narrow gauge railways, Irish narrow gauge lines are extinct, save for a few short segments used as tourist railways and a few short industrial lines.

NARROW GAUGE PHOTOGRAPHY

by John Gruber

Photography and mountain railroading go hand in hand. In Colorado, almost as soon as a new route opened, railroad companies hired skilled professionals to show off the spectacular scenery and promote travel.

Some of William Henry Jackson's narrow gauge views are almost as famous as the locations themselves. For example, the photo of the passenger train high in the Animas Canyon on the Denver & Rio Grande's Silverton Line has been seen far and wide. The Colorado Central's Georgetown Loop runs a close second. These and many others have been reproduced in a wide range of black and white and Photochrome color formats, and retouched to add trains and more dramatic backgrounds.

Jackson, the well-known Western photographer who earlier made views of Yellowstone Park for the U.S. government, opened a studio in Denver in November 1879. He started his railroad work as the D&RG opened its line through the Royal Gorge in 1880. By the end of the year, his photographs were on display in the office of F. C. Nims, general passenger agent. "One particularly surpasses the others, and a better representation of one of the best views on the great scenic line of America could not have been chosen," the *Rocky Mountain News* reported. He also prepared views of the gorge for R. F. Weibrec, D&RG treasurer.

William Henry Jackson was hired by several western railroads to photograph the building and operation of trains. He particularly favored trains in spectacular scenery. Here he pointed his camera toward a train running along the rim of the Toltec Gorge. Library of Congress, Prints and Photographs Division, Detroit Publishing Company Collection

Jackson set out from Denver in June 1881 with Thomas Moran, an artist, Ernest Ingersoll, a writer, and "Apple Jack" Karst, an engraver, for a visit to the San Juan mining region in southwestern Colorado; the D&RG's line was open to Durango and graded to Silverton. By April 1882, results of their work were evident: Ingersoll's report on the "Silver San Juan," illustrated by Moran's drawings and Karst's engravings, appeared in *Harper's New Monthly Magazine*. The journey provided Ingersoll with the opening chapters of his popular travel book, *The Crest of the Continent*, published in 1885.

Moran's drawing of Toltec Gorge, based on a Jackson photograph made at the bottom of the gorge, appeared in *Harper's Weekly*, also in 1882, with text proclaiming that the D&RG's line "runs through a region of country which presents features of grandeur unsurpassed in any other part of the world." Many times Jackson sold the same view with a train and the portal of Rock Tunnel retouched into the upper corner. Jackson had accompanied a newspaper editor's train in October 1880 to the then end of the line at Toltec Gorge, the first excursion on the trackage, and returned about a week later for pictures of the scenery. Nims, as he had done many other times, provided a railroad car for Jackson to live in while making the photographs.

The Silverton Line opened in July 1882. Jackson moved his large camera to the bottom of the canyon in 1883 to make the famous view of the train along the rock ledge, high above the rushing waters.

Jackson continued the photographic work as the D&RG opened more routes, while covering other narrow gauge lines as well: Colorado Central, 1884, 1885, 1889; Denver South Park & Pacific, 1885, 1886; Florence & Cripple Creek, 1894; and Rio Grande Southern, 1892. Jackson moved to Detroit in 1897, taking his negatives with him to the Detroit Publishing Company, where many were reissued in the colorized Photochrome versions.

George E. Mellen, F. A. Nims, and A. W. Dennis also issued stereos of scenes along the D&RG. Dennis was the D&RG's official photographer for the stretch of road from Red Cliff to Glenwood Springs in 1884–1885.

Jackson's Georgetown Loop photos, altered or retouched many times, remained popular for years. The most popular, from high on the mountainside overlooking the spindly bridge, was made in 1885, a year after the loop opened.

The loop provided the opportunity for an early experiment, the attempt of Harry Buckwater of Denver to photograph it from a balloon in 1901. The Colorado and Southern, successor to the Colorado Central, hired Buckwater and balloonist Ivy Baldwin to make the aerial view, but moments after they started out, the balloon was torn by high winds and crashed. Buckwater was forced to stay on firm ground for his work.

Records at the Colorado Railroad Museum show that for a Jackson expedition in December 1892, the Rio Grande Southern "paid man at Ophir for hauling camera up mountain $1.50," and include time sheets for a 4-4-0, No. 36, running "special service" to Lizard Head. An accompanying panoramic photo by Jackson shows the same two-car train five times at locations on the Ophir Loop; the negatives were carefully blended together when printed so the seams did not show.

Fred Jukes, a railroader who worked as a telegrapher at Chama and many other locations in the West, photographed the narrow gauge early in the twentieth century. A tall pine tree next to the tracks just east of Chama is often called the Jukes Tree, since it frequently appeared in Jukes's photos.

The times of expansion had ended, but travel promotion continued. George L. Beam took over photo duties for the D&RG in 1898, and continued as company photographer until 1935. Rio Grande maintained coverage of narrow gauge activities; photos of the last D&RGW rotary snowplow at Cumbres Pass appear in its company newspaper, *Green Light,* in 1962.

Today, tourist railroads operate at three highly ranked scenic spots—Animas Canyon, Toltec Gorge, and Georgetown. Where in the 1880s one photographer would have carried heavy equipment long distances for a single photograph, scores of rail enthusiasts now record the passing of trains.

William Henry Jackson's famous photo of the Georgetown Loop. It was taken as a black and white image using a large format glass plate. Later prints were hand tinted. Library of Congress, Prints and Photographs Division, Detroit Publishing Company Collection

Chapter 2

RIO GRANDE NARROW GAUGE

The Colorado Rockies are both an obstacle and a treasure; they present a formidable barrier to transportation, but are also one of the foremost scenic splendors in the United States, with a wealth of natural resources. During the 1850s and 1860s, when railroad surveyors were planning the route for the first transcontinental railroad (built

Denver & Rio Grande visionary, William Jackson Palmer. When Palmer proposed his Denver & Rio Grande, a line designed to connect Denver with Santa Fe and Mexico City, Denver was but a frontier village with a population of approximately 5,000 people. Santa Fe and Mexico City, on the other hand, were long-established population centers, so it's no wonder Palmer looked south. Denver Public Library, Western History Department

Previous pages
The building of the Rio Grande opened up the region to industry and agriculture. Prior to the advent of the railroad, the high cost of transportation in the region prohibited most economic activity. At Lobato—340 miles from Denver—Rio Grande K-27 climbs eastbound toward Cumbres Pass with a photographers' special on June 24, 1995. photo by Brian Jennison

by the Union Pacific and Central Pacific), they looked at running the line through the central Rockies, but decided it was not cost effective. Instead, the first transcontinental line missed Colorado entirely, and took an easier route via Cheyenne, Wyoming, and over Sherman Hill, just a few miles west of Cheyenne.

Enthusiastic citizens of Denver, an expanding village located at the foot of the Front Range, who hoped for a railway connection to the East, were disappointed and outraged when they learned Denver would not enjoy the great benefits of mainline railroad transportation. Despite being missed by the first transcontinental, by 1870 two railway lines reached Denver—a branch south from the Union Pacific mainline at Cheyenne, and a second line west from Kansas City.

The latter, the Kansas Pacific, employed one of the great American railroad visionaries: Union General William Jackson Palmer. The farsighted, talented Palmer was among the most ambitious men of his generation. He was educated in England, and prior to the Civil War he worked for J. Edgar Thompson, the illustrious president of the Pennsylvania Railroad. Under the direction of men like Thompson, the Pennsylvania Railroad became one of the foremost transportation companies in the United States, on its way to becoming one of the most powerful corporations in the world. Undoubtedly, working for this dynamic organization set Palmer's standards high.

Before the Kansas Pacific had even reached Denver, Palmer envisioned building a railroad southward along the Colorado Front Range that would tap the vast natural resources in the mountains. This goal was part of a much bigger plan—to link with transcontinental traffic on the Union Pacific and the famous Santa Fe Trail, and ultimately connect Denver with the long-established trading centers of Santa Fe and distant Mexico City. He was not alone in his vision to build a line to Mexico—Santa Fe Railway founder and promoter Cyrus Holiday also hoped to reach Mexico City, among other remote destinations.

Palmer approached the Kansas Pacific with his ambitious plans, but his railroad fantasy failed to interest his employer. Undaunted, he pushed the project forward himself. While on the payroll of the Kansas Pacific, Palmer went east to raise capital for his railroad project. On his way, he had a fortuitous meeting with William P. Mellen, an influential lawyer from New York traveling eastward with his attractive, eligible daughter, Mary. Sensing opportunity, Palmer explained his plan to Mellen and simultaneously began courting Mary. Palmer's charms were persuasive, for in short order he won both Mellen's support for his business plan (and through him valuable financial connections) and Mary's hand in marriage.

Palmer's personal correspondence from this formative period in his career indicates a remarkable, egalitarian viewpoint toward business and his railroad endeavors. The American West was a place of great hope and optimism, and Palmer had visions of building a utopian society. He wanted to make a better life for himself, his family, and his employees. He believed in treating workers justly and giving them fair compensation for their labors. Robert Athearn, in his book *Rebel of the Rockies*, quotes from a letter of Palmer's: "Each and all [employees] should feel as if it were their business and that they were adding to their store and growing more prosperous along with the road."

This attitude set him apart from many of his contemporaries in business. Nevertheless, despite these benevolent intentions, he saw no contradiction in enjoying his position and profits by living a life of royalty.

William Jackson Palmer married Mary Lincoln Mellen in Autumn 1870 and sailed to Britain for an extended honeymoon. While in Britain, Palmer visited North Wales on the advice of an associate to inspect the 2-foot gauge slate-hauling Festiniog

In the autumn of 1870, Palmer went to visit the 2-foot gauge, slate-hauling Festiniog Railway in Wales. Narrow gauge railways were significantly cheaper to build than standard gauge lines in mountainous terrain. The Festiniog, pictured here, was in many ways the inspiration for Palmer's Denver Rio Grande, although he adopted a slightly wider 3-foot gauge for his railway.

Railway. There he met with Robert Fairlie, one of the leading narrow gauge proponents and a narrow gauge designer, who advised Palmer on railroad building. What Palmer learned in Wales had a profound impact on his railroading plans.

How Wide the Tracks?

The roots of the modern railway can be traced to quarries and collieries in England and Wales, where horse-drawn tram lines had existed for generations to haul stone and coal from the mines. The steam locomotive was introduced on the Pen-y-Darren colliery in Wales in 1803, where pioneering designer Richard Trevithick demonstrated his first full-size locomotive.

The jump from singular-purpose, industrial tram railway to a public steam railway occurred more than two decades later when George

Fairlie locomotive David Lloyd George *leads a Festiniog train upgrade in the mountains of Wales near Dduallt. Robert Fairlie was among the most ardent promoters of narrow gauge railroading. He designed a distinctive type of double-ended locomotive that was very popular on some narrow gauge railways, including Festiniog. Palmer purchased a single Fairlie for the Denver & Rio Grande, but it was not well received.*

Stephenson's Stockton & Darlington line debuted in 1825. This historic railway helped establish track width of 4 feet, 8 1/2 inches as British standard gauge. Stephenson is believed to have chosen this track width because it was a common gauge used on many tram lines. (Some scholars even believe that this width dates back to Roman imperial times, as the gauge used by Roman chariots to conquer Europe.) Regardless of lineage, the Stockton & Darlington set the precedent, and most subsequent lines in England, as well as many in Continental Europe and in America, followed suit with 4-foot, 8-1/2-inch tracks.

As with just about every railway standard, there were notable exceptions. Isabard Kingdom Brunel, the famed British engineer of bridges, ships, and railways, vocally objected to Stephenson's standard, calling it unsuitable for the sort of railway he envisioned—a high-speed line, designed to handle trains moving as fast as 60 miles per hour. Brunel referred to Stephenson's standard as "narrow gauge" and used a 7-foot "broad gauge" on his Great Western Railway. In America, some lines also adopted gauges different from the Stephenson standard. Most notably, the Erie Railroad used 6-foot gauge, and the St.

Lawrence & Atlantic used 5-foot, 6-inch gauge. And while most public railways in England used the Stephenson standard, narrower gauges were still employed on many tram railways, especially where larger track widths weren't cost effective.

Festiniog Railway

During the 1830s, the narrow gauge Festiniog Railway was constructed, connecting the slate mining town of Blaenau Ffestiniog (the town is usually spelled with two "f"s, while the railway is often spelled with just one), to Porthmadog (Port Madoc), a seaside port developed especially for slate export. In its first three decades, the Festiniog was a tram railway, operating loaded trains by gravity and hauling empty wagons back up to the mines with horses. Two-foot gauge (actually 1 foot, 11 1/2 inches, with some authorities stating a more precise figure of 1 foot, 11 5/8 inches) was chosen because that width was better suited for the mine wagons, and permitted the unusually tight curvature needed to bring the line through the Welsh mountains without exceptional engineering. A standard gauge line would have been prohibitively expensive to build, requiring considerable cuts, fills, and tunnels. The 2-foot line required two tunnels.

While the builders of the Festiniog Railway considered using steam power early in its history, the prevailing philosophy of the 1840s and 1850s discouraged locomotives of 2-foot gauge proportions. Many builders felt that the narrow, often tightly curving track was unsuited for locomotive use. One locomotive authority even made the absurd allegation that 2-foot gauge locomotives would "topple over." Thus the railway continued for three decades to use "gravity" trains for downward-bound loads, and hauled the empty wagons back up the mountains with horses.

By the 1860s, the great success of the Welsh slate industry had seriously strained the capacity of the Festiniog Railway, forcing its management to look for ways to increase capacity. At the same time, the diminutive line was threatened by several proposed standard gauge lines. If these were completed, they might grab much of Festiniog's traffic and put the small line out of business. Locomotives appeared to be the most practical solution for improving the railway's capacity. Finally, in October 1863, after years of interest, the Festiniog introduced locomotive operation (although gravity trains continued to operate on a limited basis for many more years).

For many years, the Festiniog had been strictly a freight-hauling line, because British law prohibited railways with track gauge narrower than the Stephenson standard from carrying passengers. However, in 1864 the Festiniog was exempted from this prohibition, allowing it to begin passenger service.

The Festiniog Railway, while neither the first narrow gauge line to use steam locomotives, nor the first public narrow gauge line, was probably the most influential railway in the world in the

An upgrade Festiniog train nears the village of Blaenau Ffestiniog in the mountains of Wales. In its first three decades, the Festiniog Railway was primarily a slate hauler. It used gravity trains to deliver loads from the mines at Blaenau Ffestiniog to ships at Porthmadog. Animal power was used to bring trains upgrade. Inconsistencies in spelling "Ffestiniog" have been attributed to difficulties English businessmen encountered with the Welsh language.

formative years of narrow gauge railroading. Within a few years of the Festiniog's adoption of steam locomotives and passenger services, narrow gauge railways began regular service in India, and in the Queensland region of Australia. Another early public narrow gauge line had opened in Norway in 1862.

Narrow Gauge Advantage

When Palmer visited the Festiniog in November 1870, it was a busy and successful example of a mountain narrow gauge railway. While only 14 miles long, the Festiniog operated in terrain similar to that which Palmer hoped to conquer in Colorado.

Narrow gauge lines were cheaper to construct and operate than standard gauge lines. This was an especially important consideration when building railways that would operate over long distances in rough terrain with comparatively light traffic densities. Narrow gauge lines used lighter rail and shorter ties, which cost less than their standard gauge equivalents; but more importantly, narrow gauge trains could negotiate significantly sharper curves, and steeper grades, thus making narrow gauge railways substantially cheaper to build in mountainous regions. A narrow gauge line might wind its way through a deep mountain canyon with a bare minimum of cuts and fills, and no tunnels at all, where a standard gauge line would require substantial earth work and numerous tunnels to follow the same route. In these cases, the savings might make the difference between a cost-effective railway and one that was prohibitively expensive to build.

The Festiniog line needed two tunnels to reach its destination. An upbound train nears the first of these tunnels during a June downpour in 1998. While some slate is still mined, the Festiniog has not hauled revenue freight since the 1950s, and today the railway is operated as an excursion line.

On November 26, 1942, Rio Grande 2-8-0 Consolidation No. 317 leads a 24-car train through Cimarron Canyon near Cimarron, Colorado. Cimarron Canyon was located on the original narrow gauge mainline from Denver to Salt Lake City. This route was relegated to secondary status on completion of the standard gauge mainline via Tennessee Pass in 1890. Otto C. Perry, Denver Public Library, Western History Department

Another argument favoring narrow gauge was that the tare weight (empty weight of railway equipment) was proportionately less than standard gauge, so narrow gauge trains would require less energy to move. Again, this was an especially important concern when planning to operate trains over long, steep mountain grades.

Based on his assessment of the Festiniog, and meetings with Robert Fairlie, Palmer was convinced that the economies of narrow gauge would suit his needs in the Colorado Rockies. However, he deemed the 2-foot gauge used by the Festiniog too narrow for his applications, and instead followed the suggestion of Fairlie, who recommended using a slightly larger gauge. Palmer settled on 3-foot gauge for his Denver & Rio Grande.

Dawn of a Narrow Gauge Empire

The Rio Grande was among the very earliest American railways to adopt narrow gauge. It

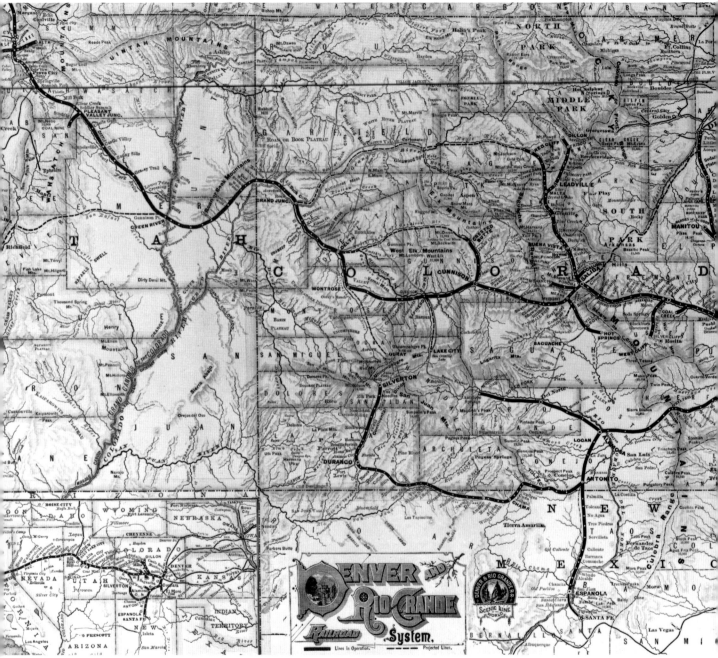

A map of Palmer's Denver & Rio Grande in 1887 shows trackage in Colorado, Utah, and New Mexico. The original 3-foot gauge mainline went via Gunnison, Montrose, and Grand Junction. The San Juan Extension runs westward from Antonito along the Colorado—New Mexico line via Antonito and Chama to Durango. The Royal Gorge, site of a heated dispute with the Santa Fe, is a few miles west of Canon City. Denver Public Library Western History Department

Rio Grande station sign marks the side of the Silverton depot. Today, Silverton is the north end of track for the Silverton Branch—the terminus of the Durango & Silverton Narrow Gauge—but 100 years ago, it was a major rail hub where three tributary lines met the Rio Grande. Silver mining was big business in Silverton during the later part of the nineteenth century.

On August 28, 1967, roughly 87 years after the San Juan Extension was built, master railroad photographer John Gruber captured the spirit of the narrow gauge's raw, remote character with this portrait of a locomotive engineer nearing Lava Tank, New Mexico, 11 miles west of Antonito, Colorado, in the open desert. John Gruber

would become the most enthusiastic builder in that gauge, and ultimately the last large American common carrier to use it.

Palmer chartered Denver & Rio Grande in October 1870 prior to leaving for Britain. During his travels he secured financing for the railway, both from Britain, where narrow gauge lines were respected, and the eastern United States, where he had good financial contacts. On returning to Colorado he wasted little time pushing the D&RG forward. In February 1871, shortly after his return, he publicly committed the D&RG to narrow gauge. Construction began with a ceremony in Denver in July 1871.

On a brisk October 28, 1871, less than a year after Palmer's visit to the Festiniog, the first Denver & Rio Grande train ran from Denver to Colorado Springs—the latter founded by Palmer as a resort community the same year, and dubbed "Little London." A small 2-4-0 named *Montezuma,* built by Baldwin and heralded as its first narrow gauge locomotive, had the honors of hauling a short trainload of dignitaries, celebrities, and

reporters over the Lake Divide. At a conservative speed of just 15 miles per hour, the 76 mile trip took 5 hours.

This was just the first step of Palmer's vision. He planned a direct line to Mexico, establishing a 3-foot gauge empire across the American Southwest with branches to tap mineral wealth in the mountains, and a westward connection with the Central Pacific. There were no other railroads in the region to compete with his 3-foot D&RG, and Palmer felt confident he would have a secure hold on rail traffic moving to and from the Rockies and points south.

Regular service on the D&RG to Colorado Springs began on January 1, 1872. Later that year the tracks reached Pueblo, 118 miles south of Denver, and a branch was constructed from Pueblo toward Canon City to tap into lucrative coal traffic. Years later, coal would later become one of Rio Grande's most profitable traffic sources. The little railway was an initial success: it carried 25,168 passengers, and approximately 46,000 tons of freight during its first year. It was

Denver & Rio Grande Western K-36 Mikado No. 489 waits to depart Antonito, Colorado, for the mountains in the west. The Rio Grande narrow gauge is an historical anomaly: it was built to satisfy transportation needs during a mining boom and to advance the business schemes of its promoter, yet it survived as a common carrier for more than 80 years, long after the development of more practical transportation systems.

held by narrow gauge promoters as the premier American narrow gauge railway. They hoped it would encourage narrow gauge construction in other parts of the country, which it did.

After a promising start, however, the D&RG suffered financial difficulties caused in part by the national economic downturn as a result of the Panic of 1873. It also fell victim to some unwise management decisions. Following its initial growth burst, the little line did not build any substantial extensions until 1876, when it began simultaneous expansion south toward coal mines near Trinidad and over La Veta Pass (called Veta Pass on some maps) to the agricultural San Luis Valley. It reached south to Trinidad in 1877 and west to Alamosa in 1878.

By that time, Palmer's Rio Grande was vying for territory with Cyrus Holliday's standard gauge Atchison, Topeka & Santa Fe, a line rapidly expanding across the Kansas and Colorado plains with visions of tapping into the Colorado mineral traffic on its way to California. The two lines became involved in a complex territorial clash, as both tried to occupy the same narrow mountain

The village of Silverton, Colorado—9,305 feet above sea level—is located where Animas Canyon widens into a broad valley. Prior to the building of the Rio Grande in the 1880s, it languished from inadequate transportation. Towering mountains surrounding it made Silverton difficult to reach, and the deep, twisting, narrow Animas River canyon provided the only practical path to it from the south.

passes. First, the AT&SF beat Palmer's line over the crucial Raton Pass crossing, located strategically on the Colorado—New Mexico state line. Following this defeat, the D&RG, which was suffering from inadequate financing and poor planning, succumbed to a lease to the AT&SF. This, however, was not the end of the D&RG by any means.

Competition between the two lines was heightened by the prospect of reaching the booming mining community at Leadville, Colorado, which had begun to produce record amounts of precious ores. After a series of complex legal battles, political maneuvering, corporate espionage, and outright gun battles involving armed private militia, Palmer wrested the D&RG away from the Santa Fe. Yet he never regained full financial control of his line.

Corporate financier and notorious railroad magnate Jay Gould bought a controlling interest in Palmer's narrow gauge and, in 1880, dictated the terms of a settlement—known as the Treaty of Boston—between the D&RG, Santa Fe, and Union Pacific (which had also become entangled in the Colorado railroad wars). With this resolution Palmer was again directing the affairs of the D&RG, but his goals had been redirected. Among other things, the treaty prohibited D&RG's southward ambitions and kept Santa Fe out of the Leadville mining district for a period of 10 years.

Palmer's Narrow Gauge Expands

While Palmer's dreams of a through line to Mexico were never realized, the years following the Treaty of Boston were D&RG's most ambitious

Morning mists clear and reveal Rio Grande narrow gauge right of way over Tennessee Pass near Pando, Colorado. When Rio Grande built its standard gauge mainline from Denver to Salt Lake City, it favored its Tennessee Pass route over the earlier narrow gauge mainline crossing at Marshall Pass. But when it rebuilt its line over Tennessee Pass, it graded a new alignment, bypassing some portions of its narrow gauge originally constructed there to reach mines at Red Cliff.

period of narrow gauge expansion. The railway simultaneously built in several directions to reach new traffic sources. Narrow gauge forged up the Royal Gorge of the Arkansas—where the D&RG forces had battled with the Santa Fe— reaching Salida in 1880 and the Leadville mining district in 1881. A branch was pushed over the 10,000-foot Tennessee Pass to reach a mining community at Red Cliff. Another route was constructed westward from Salida over Marshall Pass, reaching the Gunnison mining area, Montrose, and Grand Junction in 1881. This line became the narrow gauge mainline to the west.

A separate company controlled by Palmer, called the Denver & Rio Grande Western, was incorporated in Utah and built to the Great Salt Lake. The D&RGW absorbed existing narrow gauge railways and reached Salt Lake City in the spring of 1883, and later that year it reached a few miles farther north to a connection with the Central Pacific at Ogden. Westward from Antonito, a line known as the San Juan Extension was built over Cumbres Pass. It reached Durango, Colorado, in 1881. A branch was built up the Animas River to the mining town of Silverton. Numerous other short branches were constructed off these main trunks. Palmer also continued to push his narrow gauge southward and finally reached Santa Fe, New Mexico, in the 1890s.

Rio Grande K-27 No. 463 belches smoke on a warm September afternoon. Narrow gauge railways were built across Colorado, Utah, and New Mexico at a tremendous rate during the late 1870s and 1880s, and Rio Grande was one of several 3-foot gauge lines in the Rockies.

Against the glow of a summer morning sun, a Rio Grande Mikado leads the San Juan Express *along the Animas River north of Durango, Colorado. The narrow gauge follows the Animas River for more than 45 miles between Durango and Silverton.*

The rapid growth of Palmer's Rio Grande coincided with the Colorado mining boom, and narrow gauge had a crucial symbiotic relationship with mining communities. By providing comparatively inexpensive transportation, the railroad facilitated mining in remote regions previously hampered by their isolation. More lucrative mine traffic provided the economic base to fund construction of railways to such remote regions.

The arrival of the narrow gauge allowed for greater output at existing mines and permitted the development of new mines previously deemed uneconomical because of prohibitively high transportation costs. The railroad's mine traffic consisted of heavy equipment and related mining supplies used for digging mines and refining ore; outgoing mine products in the form of coal, ore, and refined metals; the miners themselves; and products used by them and supporting industries.

Although the Rio Grande had reached many new sources of traffic, the great expense of its rapid expansion strained the company's finances and put tremendous pressure on General Palmer. Following political difficulties within the company, Palmer resigned as president of the D&RG, but remained in control of the D&RGW in Utah, leased by the D&RG. Later a serious rift between Palmer and D&RG's new management resulted in a temporary break in the narrow gauge mainline at the Colorado-Utah state line. For months the line was operated as two long, disconnected branch lines, an event that had disastrous results on traffic levels for both railways. Personality difficulties were so serious that both companies looked to find other alternatives for moving east-west traffic.

Competition

As the D&RG and D&RGW engaged in petty battles harmful to both companies, the railroad situation in the West evolved. The whole scene had changed in just a few years and had serious

Three-foot gauge tracks catch the glint of the clear morning sun at the summit of Cumbres Pass—10,016 feet above sea level. Following the "Treaty of Boston" in 1880, Palmer's Denver & Rio Grande expanded rapidly, building many new lines simultaneously, including this one over Cumbres Pass to Chama, New Mexico, and Durango.

implications for the narrow gauge mainline. By the mid-1880s, several standard gauge railways had reached Colorado, putting the Rio Grande lines in an advantageous position to haul transcontinental traffic westward to the Central Pacific at Ogden. However, gauge difference at both ends of the Rio Grande greatly increased the costs of moving transcontinental traffic. Furthermore, the Rio Grande was threatened with

On August 30, 1967, Rio Grande K-37 No. 493 rests inside the Alamosa roundhouse along with sister Mikados. After the conversion of the line over La Veta Pass to standard gauge, Alamosa was the point where narrow and standard gauge met. The railroad operated dual gauge tracks between Alamosa and Antonito. The roundhouse is gone, and today there is little evidence of the narrow gauge at Alamosa, although the town is still served by standard gauge. John Gruber

the prospect of direct competition from a standard gauge line through the Rockies.

The Colorado Midland had plans to build westward through the mountains to tap lucrative mine traffic, and possibly transcontinental traffic if it reached the Salt Lake gateway. Political difficulties between the two ends of the Rio Grande system were resolved, and by the late 1880s, the company decided to build its own standard gauge route between Denver and the Salt Lake.

This was not the first standard gauge conversion; following the Treaty of Boston the original north-south mainline had been converted to dual gauge by the addition of an outside rail. However, rather than just converting all of the existing narrow gauge mainline, Rio Grande decided on a largely new route for its standard gauge line between Salida and Grand Junction. The standard gauge line roughly traced the route of the

A brakeman's view from the caboose of a Rio Grande train on the San Juan Extension illustrates the simple, primitive nature of narrow gauge railroading. John Gruber

narrow gauge west of Grand Junction, but there were several substantial line reallocations, and the standard gauge used a new alignment designed to ease grades and curvature. Instead of going over Marshall Pass, the standard gauge mainline took a northerly path via Tennessee Pass (using a largely new alignment over the divide rather than holding tightly to the original narrow gauge alignment to Red Cliff), and then west via Glenwood Canyon.

The Denver & Rio Grande reached peak narrow gauge mileage in 1889 when it briefly operated 1,861 miles of 3-foot-gauge track (including dual gauge sections). With the completion of the standard gauge mainline in 1890, roughly 600 miles of narrow gauge were abandoned or converted.

While the conversion of the narrow gauge mainline between Denver and the Salt Lake was a symbolic defeat for the narrow gauge concept, it was not the end of the Rio Grande narrow gauge. The railroad continued to convert additional 3-foot gauge lines to standard gauge, but did not embark on a system-wide re-gauging plan; the majority of its narrow gauge network survived as built, entering a period of gradual decline, marked by boom periods when the narrow gauge was comparatively prosperous. In this respect, the Rio Grande differed from the national narrow gauge trend. In 1885, four years before D&RG's peak, the national narrow gauge route mileage peaked at 11,699 miles in service. After 1885, narrow gauge conversion to standard gauge exceeded the mileage of new narrow gauge lines built nationally.

From its beginning, the Rio Grande was the premier American narrow gauge—no other unified narrow gauge system in the United States ever approached its size. Rio Grande's loyalty to its 3-foot gauge lines caused its share of narrow gauge operations to increase as other lines around the country were abandoned or converted to standard gauge. In 1890, after the opening of its standard gauge mainline, the Rio Grande

A brakeman ties down the hand brake on top of a narrow gauge car. Traditionally, brakemen were required to ride on top of cars in order to set brakes. Prior to the introduction of the airbrake (gradually implemented between the mid-1870s and early 1890s) this was the preferred method of stopping a long train. The practice of setting brakes continued long after airbrakes were in regular use. John Gruber

narrow gauge represented nearly 15 percent of all common carrier narrow gauge lines in the United States. By 1930, despite a gradual reduction of its lines, Rio Grande operated more than 28 percent of national narrow gauge lines, and by 1953, despite substantial reductions to the Rio Grande narrow gauge system, the ratio had risen to roughly 77 percent, and it would continue to rise

Rio Grande K-36 No. 489 rolls eastward across the open desert just north of the Colorado—New Mexico line. In its haste to reach lucrative mine traffic, Rio Grande laid down its tracks right on the desert floor. As a result, the line snakes along the contour of the land to gain elevation.

until the 1960s. As a result, American narrow gauge came to be nearly synonymous with the Rio Grande.

Rio Grande clung to the narrow gauge in part because its lines were sufficiently profitable to keep open but not so lucrative as to warrant massive upgrading. This paralleled the trend in mining traffic, which initially represented a large share of the narrow gauge business, but followed the law of diminishing returns, with branches closing or being downgraded once mines were tapped out. There was little incentive to spend large sums to upgrade a line that was ultimately, like the mines it served, going to be abandoned.

Rio Grande management considered converting large portions of its narrow gauge network to standard gauge, but was hindered by chronic financial shortages. During the 1890s, the D&RG was pinched by an unstable economy and a severe decline of the silver mining industry

caused by a repeal of the Sherman Silver Purchase Act in 1893.

At the turn of the century, the railroad came under the control of George Gould, son of Jay Gould, who had briefly controlled the Rio Grande 20 years earlier. Following in the steps of his father, the younger Gould had visions of a true transcontinental railroad network that would stretch from coast to coast. (The so-called Transcontinental Railroad of 1869 was built as two companies and only stretched from eastern connections at Council Bluffs, Iowa, to California.) He was in the process of piecing together a nationwide rail system that included the Missouri Pacific and several eastern carriers when he bought into the Rio Grande. The Rio Grande played a crucial role in Gould's scheme: not only did it provide a vital link in his transcontinental plan, but he used Rio Grande profits for the building of a new railroad from Salt Lake City to Oakland called the Western Pacific.

The siphoning of Rio Grande profits may have been necessary to fulfill Gould's vision, but it had disastrous implications for the Rio Grande. Money that could have been used for improvements, maintenance, and other projects on the Rio Grande instead were directed toward funding an 800-mile branch railroad to California. The Rio Grande suffered from neglect, experiencing numerous accidents, including several horrible collisions that killed dozens of people. During this time, Palmer relinquished his last holdings in the Rio Grande, and in 1908 the Denver & Rio Grande and the Rio Grande Western (the name of the Utah lines after 1889) were finally merged.

Following his retirement, Palmer is said to have distributed nearly a million dollars in bonuses to choice railroad employees—a benevolent act consistent with his attitudes. Yet he was highly critical of the Rio Grande under Gould's influence and complained about the railroad's deteriorating condition.

The Western Pacific was completed to the West Coast, but Gould fell short of building his transcontinental railway system, and lost control of his empire on the eve of American involvement in the first World War. Following the war and the government control of railroads during that period, the Denver & Rio Grande was reorganized as the Denver & Rio Grande Western Railroad (not to be confused with Palmer's Utah narrow gauges that were operated as the Denver & Rio Grande Western Railway) to free it from financial entanglement with Western Pacific.

During this period, there were only a few changes to the narrow gauge lines. Although narrow gauge mileage faced slow decline, there were some new additions: in 1923, the isolated standard gauge branch from Durango, Colorado, to Farmington, New Mexico, which had been constructed some years earlier in part to thwart encroachment of the Southern Pacific into Rio

The timeless quality of the narrow gauge is its greatest appeal. It takes you back decades to a time when steam locomotives ruled the land, and the train— even when plodding along at just 12 to 15 miles per hour—was the best and fastest way to go. Mikado No. 489 rolls eastward toward Antonito.

Rio Grande depot at Chama, New Mexico. Located at the base of the grade over Cumbres Pass and situated roughly midway between Alamosa and Durango, Chama was ideally situated for a railway terminal. It served as an "away terminal" and crews would typically operate in both directions to Chama. Today, it is the base of operations for the Cumbres & Toltec Scenic Railroad.

Grande territory, was converted to 3-foot gauge. Rio Grande's core narrow gauge network remained largely intact through the end of World War II. But after the war, the narrow gauge system was viewed as obsolete and was gradually dismembered over the next 20 years. In 1949 the famed narrow gauge circle was broken when 27 miles of the old narrow gauge Utah mainline between Cedar Creek and Saphiero, Colorado, over Cerro Summit were abandoned. In 1952, the Rio Grande Southern succumbed to abandonment. This 3-foot-gauge Rio Grande subsidiary had made up the west end of the circle and connected to the D&RGW at Durango and Ridgway by way of the legendary Lizard Head Pass crossing in southwestern Colorado.

During the next few years, the Rio Grande continued to whittle away at its narrow gauge network. By 1956, following the conversion of its profitable Monarch branch (roughly 21 miles running from Salida to Monarch via Poncha Junction and Maysville) to standard gauge operation, only the San Juan Extension from Alamosa to Durango and the branches from Durango to Silverton and Farmington remained of Palmer's once vast narrow gauge empire. This isolated narrow gauge remnant survived roughly intact as a Class I common carrier operation for another dozen years.

It is the San Juan extension that is the best remembered, most documented, and certainly the best preserved segment of the Rio Grande narrow gauge.

Rio Grande K-37—D&RGW's largest and most powerful class of narrow gauge Mikado—strains as it ascends the 4 percent grade over Cumbres Pass with maximum tonnage. The train would lose traction and stall twice before reaching the summit. Eastbound freight trains were often brought from Chama to Cumbres in several sections and then assembled into one consist for the trip to Alamosa.

A train climbing toward Cumbres Pass can be heard long before it is seen. Rio Grande No. 497 has just passed milepost 333 near Coxo—nearly 9,750 feet above sea level and 2.5 track miles from the summit, but less than a mile as the crow flies. Coxo was once the location of an 800-foot siding, just long enough to hold a short train.

Heavy excursion trains require a helper from Chama up the 4 percent grade to Cumbres Pass. On Saturday, September 5, 1998, Mud hen No. 463 works as a headend helper at Cresco Tank. At Cumbres Pass it will cut off, run around the summit wye, and return to Chama light. Before World War I, the D&RG upgraded the west slope of Cumbres Pass with heavier track specifically to permit operation of its K-27 Mud hens as helpers.

Chapter 3

THE SAN JUAN EXTENSION

The two tourist lines now known respectively as the Cumbres & Toltec Scenic and the Durango & Silverton Narrow Gauge were once parts of Rio Grande's San Juan Extension—just one portion of William Jackson Palmer's vast narrow gauge empire that covered much of western Colorado,

Rio Grande Mikados Nos. 489 and 463 lead a photographer's special westward through Tanglefoot Curve near the summit of Cumbres Pass in July 1998. Cumbres & Toltec occasionally runs vintage freight trains that nearly replicate operations of an earlier era. John Gruber

Previous pages
Near Dalton, New Mexico, in September 1996, Cumbres & Toltec No. 488 leads the daily excursion train eastbound up the 4 percent grade toward Cumbres Pass. Cumbres & Toltec operates excursions between May and October on this scenic mountain crossing.

northern New Mexico, and parts of Utah. Today, these surviving narrow gauge segments are the only substantial narrow gauge remnants of the Rio Grande narrow gauge system, and two of the longest remaining narrow gauge lines in the United States. (Many other former D&RGW narrow gauge lines survive as standard gauge routes.)

Early on, Palmer had planned to build a branch to the San Juan district, but his route there evolved as events in Colorado railroading altered the Rio Grande's route. Ultimately, the

Rio Grande built westward from Antonito. It followed the north side of the Toltec Gorge, crossed Cumbres Pass—a 10,015 foot crossing east of the continental divide—then dropped down to Chama, New Mexico, before climbing again, surmounting the divide, and descending into the Animas River Valley to reach the new town of Durango, Colorado.

Rio Grande's entry into the region had been delayed by insufficient financing and problems with its standard gauge competitors, but following the Treaty of Boston it built at a furious pace. The railroad more than doubled in size during 1880. Numerous track crews graded and laid down nearly 350 miles of line, more track than had been built during Rio Grande's first 8 years.

Eager to tap into profitable new silver traffic and fend off competition from other lines, Rio Grande management rushed to complete the San Juan extension. Its sinuous routing reflects Rio Grande's inexpensive, hasty construction. The railroad follows natural contours of the land—winding around, often looping back on itself to maintain an even gradient, while gaining elevation—rather than using many costly deep cuts

Cumbres & Toltec fireman in period dress leans from the cab of K-36 No. 487 at Chama, New Mexico, in September 1996.

Cumbres & Toltec No. 484 pauses at the water tank in Antonito, Colorado. Water tanks are spotted at key locations along the railroad to insure locomotives always have sufficient water in the boiler. If a locomotive runs low on water, there is a risk of a boiler explosion.

In late September and early October brightly colored aspens attract thousands of visitors to Colorado and northern New Mexico. This is one of the busiest times of year for the Cumbres & Toltec. An excursion rolls along the Toltec Gorge during peak color in 1994. Hal Miller

and high fills. The line was built using very light-weight rail, usually 30 pounds per yard, then the standard on most Rio Grande narrow gauge lines, and simple dirt-and-cinder ballast.

Tracks crossed Cumbres Pass in July 1880, reached Chama, New Mexico, at the end of 1880, and arrived in Durango, Colorado, in July 1881. A year later, a branch up the narrow, deep Animas canyon to Silverton was completed. Considering

Opposite
Steam locomotives require hours of labor-intensive preparation before they are ready to operate. Cumbres & Toltec crews clean the ashpans on Mikado No. 489 in Chama, New Mexico. Scenes like this were once common in small town engine terminals all across America.

Beneath a radiant blue dome, Rio Grande K-37 works the 4 percent grade at Dalton, New Mexico. Today's train is particularly heavy and the locomotive is working extra hard.

the rough terrain and the great number of other construction projects the Rio Grande was undertaking, the rapidity of construction to Durango was remarkable. In October 1880, just a few days after the tracks were completed to Chama, the Rio Grande ran a special passenger excursion over the new line for the benefit of journalists, local dignitaries, and the noted railway photographer, William Henry Jackson.

Durango, like other new towns along the railroad, arose largely through Rio Grande interests. It was founded near the existing community of Animas City just prior to the arrival of tracks from Antonito. When the railroad opened, Durango boomed and soon dwarfed the importance of its older neighbor. In time, Durango became a significant railroad hub. Featuring a freight yard and roundhouse, it was the western base of operation for the San Juan extension, and a major junction point. The Silverton Branch continued north along the Animas River and another branch went south to Farmington, New Mexico. Durango was also the southern connection with the Rio Grande Southern.

The completion of the San Juan Extension precipitated a mining boom, and the whole region flourished with new economic activities— a common pattern following the growth of the Rio Grande in Colorado and New Mexico. Western railroad and mining boom towns were notoriously uncivilized places. Lined with saloons, gambling halls, and brothels, these budding communities attracted an amoral, unsavory lot of people: men seeking their fortune through personal labor, business schemes, gambling, or whatever other methods seemed appropriate.

The tallest bridge on the Cumbres & Toltec is the Cascade Trestle, located near milepost 320, west of Osier, Colorado. The 408-foot long, 137-foot tall bridge crosses Cascade Creek 9,630 feet above sea level. John Gruber photographed K-27 No. 463 with a photographers' special on July 25, 1998. John Gruber

Their activities left legends of debauchery, lawlessness, violence, and colorful antics.

Railroad lore from this region is filled with stories from this unique period of American history. The line over Cumbres Pass has its fair share of tales. Just a few miles west of Antonito is a small wooden bridge popularly known as Hangman's trestle. Apparently, in the early days of the railroad, vigilantes stole a locomotive from the Antonito yard in order to bring their victim to this bridge for execution. There were few suitable trees for the purpose, and perhaps the vigilantes preferred a more remote spot to dispense rough justice.

Traffic and Operations

Although mine traffic precipitated the line's construction, mine products represented only a portion of freight carried over the line. Agricultural products, timber, and incoming manufactured goods were also important sources of revenue. West of Chama, significant timber operations sponsored several railroad spurs, branches, and connecting short lines. These were variously operated by the railroad and other firms, such as New Mexico Lumber Company, Pagosa Lumber Company, and others.

After the turn of the century, new industries developed along the line and the Rio Grande was rewarded with new, previously unanticipated traffic sources. Ironically, the growth of motorized highway transport—an industry that ultimately doomed the Rio Grande narrow gauge—provided the railroad with considerable new traffic during its last three decades.

During the 1930s, the development of the Gramps oil field, located between Chama and Pagosa Springs, produced considerable new business.

Durango & Silverton operates through a remote section of the Animas Canyon that is not accessible by road. In September 1998, a Durango-bound train negotiates the winding track near the lower end of the Animas Canyon.

The wye at Big Horn, located 9,022 feet above sea level just south of the Colorado—New Mexico line, basks in the glow of the full moon. At night, the rails over Cumbres Pass are quiet. Traditionally, when the railroad operated as a common carrier, trains ran night and day. Today, excursions usually operate in daylight.

For nearly 30 years, Rio Grande profited by hauling train loads of tank cars filled with crude oil from a pipeline transfer depot in Chama to a refinery in Alamosa. After 1936, it was common to see long trains of black cylindrical Union Tank Car Company cars on Rio Grande's freights winding their way over Cumbres Pass.

The popularity of motorized transport grew and demand for oil rapidly increased, resulting in extensive oil exploration in the American West. In the 1950s, oil and natural gas fields were developed in the vicinity of Farmington, New Mexico, and for a few years the once-sleepy Farmington Branch boomed with new oil-field traffic. For several years

The narrow gauge was simply and cheaply built. Tracks were often laid down with minimal roadbed or ballast. In places, the tracks are visible only to the careful observer. The Big Horn Wye catches the glint of the rising summer sun.

Rio Grande moved large daily trains, sometimes up to 70 cars long, carrying pipe and drilling equipment over Cumbres Pass to Chama and Durango, then down the Farmington Branch to the new oil fields. Rio Grande carried an estimated 6,000 carloads of oil-field pipe during the 1950s. Prior to the oil-field boom, the meandering Farmington Branch was known for its infrequent short freights, often only two or three cars long.

Taken in June 1995—but looking like a scene from the mid-1950s—K-27 463 leads a photographers' special upgrade at Coxo Curve not far from Cumbres Pass. Brian Jennison

The toughest part of the San Juan Extension has always been the long 4 percent grade ascending the west slope of Cumbres Pass, where the tracks climb 2,152 feet in just 13 miles between Chama and the summit. During the early days of operation this lightly built railroad with its tortuous, steeply graded profile could only accommodate comparatively short freight trains. Two of Rio Grande's larger Consolidation-type locomotives (those delivered between 1878 and 1882) were generally assigned to a 12- to 15-car freight. At Chama, an additional two Consolidations would be added as helpers for the tough ascent of Cumbres Pass.

The San Juan Extension's lightweight construction made it a bastion of antique equipment. Light rail, cinder ballast, and primitive bridges prohibited the use of newer, heavier locomotives on the line. Shortly before World War I, Rio Grande improved the west slope of Cumbres Pass with heavier rail specifically to accommodate the K27 Mikados, then Rio Grande's most powerful narrow gauge locomotives, but already a decade old. The big engines were limited to helper service on the 4 percent climb to the summit. The rest of the route was upgraded during the mid-1920s to accommodate the new (and even larger) K28 and K36 Mikados, locomotives that dominated late-era Rio Grande narrow gauge operations.

Train crews would operate from both Durango and Alamosa to Chama, located roughly midway between the two home terminals. Eastbound trains out of Durango were often "doubleheaded" (meaning two locomotives were used), and additional helpers might be added at Chama for the steep climb up the Cumbres Pass on the way to Alamosa. It was common practice to split the locomotives on heavy trains from Alamosa, placing one mid-train. Separating the heavy engines by a number of lighter-weight cars reduced drawbar strain on the lead locomotive, which was especially severe because of the exceptionally tight curvature, and minimized stress on bridges along the line. The second locomotive would be cut out, or removed from the train, on reaching the summit at Cumbres Pass and would "run light" (without a train) to the base of the grade at Chama. Considerable traffic originated at Chama, and trains operating east of Chama, hav-

Durango & Silverton excursion trains thrill passengers with a spectacular view of the deep, narrow Animas River Canyon. A southbound train hugs the shelf cut into the side of the cliff high above the rushing water of the river below.

ing additional cars, were often much heavier than those coming in from Durango.

Decline and Demise

By the mid-1950s, the San Juan Extension and its branches were the last surviving Rio Grande narrow gauge operations. The rest of the narrow gauge system had been either converted to standard gauge or abandoned. When the narrow gauge was built, it was a significant transportation improvement and proved vastly superior to the poor mountain trails that preceded it. Until the 1920s, there were few roads in the region, and the railroad was the preferred method of travel for more than half a century. However, as new roads were built and improved, the narrow gauge suffered. Despite the traditional appeal of train travel and the spectacular scenery along the route, passengers fled the rails.

The Rio Grande had operated a first class train, called the *San Juan*—complete with a luxury parlor car—between Durango and Alamosa. It made a cross-platform connection with a standard gauge passenger train to Denver at Alamosa. During the Great Depression, the railroad renewed its commitment to its narrow gauge passengers by overhauling the service and remodeling the train. And despite a general decline in patronage, narrow gauge ridership experienced a brief renaissance during World War II when gasoline and rubber tire rationing forced travelers to return to the rails. But following the war, the downward trend continued. The narrow gauge could not compete effectively with new highway services: the train took a little more than 9 hours to complete its 200-mile run (the eastbound run took slightly longer than its westbound counterpart because of the grueling 4 percent climb east of Chama), sig-

Durango & Silverton K-36 No. 480 leads a southbound train along a narrow shelf above Shalona Lake, a short distance from Rockwood, Colorado.

nificantly longer than a comparable journey over the roadways. In 1951, the railroad discontinued its famous *San Juan*—the last scheduled, named narrow gauge passenger train—leaving the tri-weekly Durango to Silverton mixed train as the only remaining passenger service.

Although the once-lucrative ore business had nearly dried up, and timber traffic had dwindled, freight traffic remained fairly robust through the 1950s because of the oil-field boom. Year-round, the railroad operated long daily freights between Alamosa and Durango. In addition to pipeline and crude oil, the railroad continued to move coal, live animals, and some merchandise traffic. Yet by 1960 much of the oil-field traffic had vanished, and in 1963 the railroad lost the Chama-to-Alamosa oil business. Daily service over the line had ended by the early 1960s, and by 1963 traffic only warranted one or two trips per week from Alamosa to Durango.

Although the railroad was obviously in decline, in 1961 and 1962 11 miles of new narrow gauge railroad were constructed between Chama and Durango because of a forced line relocation to make way for the Navajo Dam on the San Juan River in northern New Mexico, which flooded the old right-of-way. The new route was 3.5 miles longer than the original line, and opened September 13, 1962.

By the mid-1960s, the railroad estimated that the average freight car took 20 hours to move between Alamosa and Durango, nearly four times as long as typical over-the-road trucking. Furthermore, the highway distance was 50 miles shorter than the railroad. Keeping the railroad open through the winter was a costly, labor-intensive endeavor, and in the mid-1960s exceptionally harsh weather conditions and a relative dearth of freight prompted the railroad to suspend costly year-round operations over Cumbres Pass. For a few years, freight service continued on an as-needed basis during warmer seasons,

Climbing the steep grade toward Cumbres Pass, a double-headed excursion train crosses the grade crossing at Dalton, New Mexico. Watching a heavy train ascend this grade is among the most spectacular shows in American railroading.

but traffic levels continued to plummet. In 1965, the railroad moved just 1,806 narrow gauge cars, and by 1967 this figure had fallen to just 757.

In September 1967, Rio Grande applied to the Interstate Commerce Commission (ICC) to abandon its remaining narrow gauge lines, except for the 45-mile Durango to Silverton branch. A press release issued September 18th summed up the railroad's position:

> Rio Grande officials said losses on the route run above a half-million dollars a year, while the need for its services has dwindled to near the vanishing point. Only two freight trains were run over the lines in each direction in the month of August as virtually all shipping in the area was handled by highway.

The press release continued:

> The public need for transportation of freight and passengers is now and for many years past has been adequately served by highway, and the public convenience and necessity does not require continued operations of the [narrow gauge lines].

The railroad's conclusion was blunt:

> The narrow gauge is hopelessly incapable of performing competitively with modern modes of transportation and cannot approach the standards of convenience, reliability and speeds demanded for 1967 and henceforth.

The ICC examined Rio Grande's abandonment request, and despite protests, it agreed with the railroad's conclusions. In the summer of 1969, the ICC approved the abandonment of the remaining narrow gauge lines, save the popular Silverton Branch. In its report on the abandonment, the ICC found the narrow gauge railroad as "an obsolete and misfit facility wholly inadequate to meet the real needs of the communities involved."

After almost 100 years, William Jackson Palmer's narrow gauge railway finally concluded its role as a public transportation system. Looking back at its long, troubled history, it's amazing that his narrow gauge empire survived as long as it did. Nevertheless, other North American narrow gauge lines—notably the White Pass & Yukon operating in Alaska and British Columbia, and lines in the Canadian Maritime provinces—outlasted Palmer's pioneering line and survived as common carriers for another decade. While the Rio Grande narrow gauge ceased to function as a public transportation system, significant portions of the narrow gauge survived and operate today as scenic railways for the benefit of history buffs, railfans, and tourists. These lines have preserved the Rocky Mountain narrow gauge for future generations to experience and enjoy.

Silverton Branch

Silverton is an aptly named village located high in the Rockies. Founded in 1876, it served primarily as a silver mining camp, but languished because of its isolated location and high costs of transportation. With the arrival of the Rio Grande in 1882, the town thrived as a mining community. Silverton sat at the end of a remote branch on the far end of Rio Grande's vast narrow gauge empire, but in its heyday it was a major railway hub and significant traffic-gathering point.

Three different railway lines, winding down steep mountain passes from the north, fed traffic to the Rio Grande at Silverton. These lines were at various times controlled by regional transportation magnate Otto Mears, who before the arrival of the railway in southwest Colorado operated a network of toll roads. He is probably best

remembered in narrow gauge circles for his famous Rio Grande Southern, a legendary narrow gauge railway and Rio Grande subsidiary. The Silverton Railroad operated to mines near Red Mountain Pass and Ironton; the Silverton, Gladstone & Northerly Railroad connected its two namesake points, while the Silverton Northern—the last of the Silverton feeder lines built and the last to be abandoned—reached to Eureka and Animas Forks. All three lines climbed grades in excess of 5 percent, generally considered prohibitively steep for even narrow gauge main-line operations. The Silverton Northern had one short, but amazingly steep, grade of 7 percent, and trains descending this line were limited to a maximum speed of just 4 miles per hour.

Rio Grande's Silverton Branch handled a high volume of freight traffic during its first decade. But traffic dropped sharply in 1893 following the repeal of the Sherman Silver Purchase

Viewed from Windy Point, No. 489 brings an excursion train up the mountain toward Cumbres Pass on a crisp, clear October 9, 1987. The vertical scenery around the summit is particularly striking. James A. Speaker

Act, which greatly curtailed output of local silver mines. While silver mining continued, traffic levels on the branch never fully recovered. Traffic ebbed and flowed, but there was a general decline in mine traffic over the next 70 years.

A through passenger train, complete with sleeping cars, operated from Denver to Silverton via Cumbres Pass until 1893. The Silverton Branch was one of the few American narrow gauge lines to carry sleepers. The narrow gauge feeder lines to Silverton were abandoned one by one; the Silverton Railroad was nearly devoid of traffic by the end of World War I and was finally abandoned in 1922. Its tracks were lifted four years later. The Silverton, Gladstone & Northerly succumbed during the Great Depression and was abandoned in 1937 and 1938. The Silverton Northern was abandoned during World War II.

By the late 1940s, a mixed train—carrying both passengers and freight—running just three days per week was sufficient to handle rail traffic to Silverton. While Rio Grande published a schedule, the quaint little Silverton mixed didn't always adhere to the posted times. Actual running time over the line varied depending on freight movements, and the train often handled stock cars filled with live sheep loaded from trackside pens at Silverton. The mixed's departure from Silverton was dependent on the successful loading of its woolly passengers into their wooden-slatted carriages. The laid-back atmosphere in rural Colorado was quite accepting of

Cumbres & Toltec K-36 rolls eastbound toward Antonito across Hangman's Trestle at milepost 386. The open desert around Antonito presents a stark contrast to the forests along the Toltec Gorge a few miles to the west.

Previous pages
The Rio Grande followed the north rim of the Toltec Gorge to reach Cumbres Pass. This unusually spectacular route affords a tremendous view: the tracks are often hundreds of feet higher than the river. Mikado No. 484 rolls through a cut on the rim of the gorge several miles east of Sublette.

Durango & Silverton trains wind along the Animas Canyon for dozens of miles in relative seclusion from civilization. This is a beautiful, remote place best enjoyed from a narrow gauge train.

A westbound excursion train headed for Osier leaves the yard limit at Big Horn. The railroad is gradually climbing out of the desert, leaving a landscape of sagebrush to enter the mountain forest. To gain elevation, the tracks wind around: here Rio Grande engineers made use of cuts and fills to maintain a steady grade.

such loose interpretations of the schedule, and visitors would often embrace such delays as part of the narrow gauge experience.

In the early 1950s—despite years of declining fortunes on the Silverton Branch, and a nationwide trend of declining passenger ridership, particularly on rural branch line trains such as the infrequent and dawdling Silverton mixed—the Silverton line began to experience a passenger revival. People began to visit Durango specifically to ride the Silverton train. Undoubtedly, railfans and train riding enthusiasts were among the visitors, but others came too, attracted by the spectacular scenery and isolation of the Animas Canyon.

There is no highway access through most of the canyon, and it is best enjoyed from the window of a steam-powered narrow gauge train. Moreover, by the mid-1950s, the ubiquitous steam-powered passenger train—once a symbol of American prosperity—had nearly vanished from the landscape. In the 10 years since the end of World War II most American railroads had "dieselized," replacing their old, smoke-belching steam locomotives with modern diesel-electric locomotives. Some lines hung onto steam locomotives longer than others, and the Rio Grande's narrow gauge locomotives were the last large fleet of steam locomotives operated by a Class I railroad. These distinctive and nostalgic machines were no longer commonplace and were viewed as a novelty. People would gladly pay for a ride on a steam-powered passenger train.

While passenger traffic continued to grow, freight traffic plummeted. Even when other parts of the remaining Rio Grande narrow gauge lines experienced a traffic renaissance during the mid-1950s, the Silverton Branch was traffic-starved. By the late 1950s, freight traffic was nearly nonexistent. Though rumors circulated about a silver-mining resurgence and the return of lucrative mine traffic to the scenic branch, a railroad can't survive on rumors. As early as the 1940s, the railroad had hoped to discontinue service on the branch, but abandonment requests to the Interstate Commerce Commission were denied.

What preserved the Silverton Branch were the tourists. The growth in passenger ridership had proven profitable, and Rio Grande began to promote the train as a tourist attraction. The line evolved into one of the first modern tourist railways. The steam train became sufficiently popular so that in the early 1960s the railroad constructed additional narrow gauge passenger cars at its Burnham shops near Denver. To further popularize the train, the Rio Grande acquired property in Durango to build up an "Old West" theme village to entertain tourists. By 1967, Rio Grande had invested more than $2 million in the Durango & Silverton as a tourist attraction, and at that time the narrow gauge steam trains were the only profitable passenger trains on the entire railroad. Purists may have been offended by the contrived nature of the train. Its authenticity had been compromised for the sake of promotion, and it had lost much of its historical accuracy.

The Animas Canyon is many hundreds of feet deep. Toward the top of the canyon, near Silverton, the railroad is nearly at water level, but further down, the tracks rise high above the river.

In October 1995, amidst gorgeous autumn foliage, Cumbres & Toltec No. 2 (eastbound from Chama to Osier), passes Cresco Tank on its way up to Cumbres Pass. Ed Beaudette

Rio Grande Southern used a fleet of home-built railbusses known as Galloping Geese to provide passenger service over its lightly traveled lines north of Durango, Colorado. Although the RGS was abandoned in the early 1950s, most of its Geese survived. In June 1998, Goose No. 5 made a visit to the Cumbres & Toltec. It is seen at Osier meeting train No. 2. Ed Beaudette

For example, traditionally, Rio Grande painted its passenger equipment in subdued colors, usually Pullman green and black. But to better appeal to a misinformed notion of a classic western passenger train—perhaps inspired by Hollywood motion pictures and television—the cars of the Durango & Silverton were painted a brilliant yellow. For a time, other trappings, such as phony "diamond" smoke stacks, were added to locomotives, although they did not affect the performance of the engines. Despite the lack of authenticity, the public loved the D&S train and continued to flock to it.

The Durango & Silverton line was not abandoned in 1969 with the rest of the remaining narrow gauge lines, but remained as a railroad-operated tourist train. Eventually, the railroad sold the narrow gauge tourist line, and it is now privately operated for profit as the Durango & Silverton Narrow Gauge Railroad. Where a lonely mixed freight plied the rails in the early 1950s, today as

many as four daily trains operate in season to haul thousands of tourists through the Animas Canyon. It is among the most popular and most successful tourist trains in the United States.

Cumbres & Toltec

The allure of diminutive remote railroading is undeniably strong. The narrow gauge developed a greater popular following as it became an isolated, anachronistic transportation system. In 1885, there were narrow gauge railways all over the United States, but by the 1960s the surviving Rio Grande narrow gauge was viewed as a quaint, historical curiosity. As railroads faded in importance, insightful individuals began to preserve elements for posterity.

Since World War II, numerous efforts have been undertaken around the country to preserve railway history, and narrow gauge preservation was among the earliest concerns. During the 1950s, Robert Richardson collected narrow gauge

Cumbres & Toltec's Leslie Rotary snowplow OY digs into the drifts west of Cumbres, Colorado, on May 7, 1997. A steam-powered rotary snow plow at work is one of the most spectacular sights in railroading. Joe McMillan

equipment, including a steam locomotive, and his collection later became the basis for the Colorado Railroad Museum—now located at Golden, Colorado. By the late 1960s, the Rio Grande narrow gauge had an international following. Thousands of people had come world round to ride the Durango & Silverton, and numerous books covered the narrow gauge story. The Rio Grande 3-foot gauge had survived long enough for its historical significance to be recognized.

In 1967, when the Denver, Rio Grande & Western made its abandonment announcement, an established railway preservation community in the United States was ready to act. Some early efforts intended to preserve the remaining narrow gauge in its entirety; these efforts failed, but the railroad's historical value warranted national attention. The National Park Service even entertained preserving the railroad, but decided against it. Finally, as abandonment loomed, New

Mexico and Colorado formed independent railroad authorities aimed at saving portions of the line. Ultimately, the two states joined to purchase the 64-mile line segment from Antonito, Colorado, to Chama, New Mexico. In July 1970, the states acquired the line and the Cumbres & Toltec Scenic Railroad was formed.

That summer, a team of dedicated volunteers began improving the property to reopen the line, which had suffered from years of neglect. A year had passed since the Rio Grande operated its last revenue train, and in places mud and rocks had buried the tracks. By September, the line was opened so equipment could be moved from Antonito to Chama—an imperative move because the railroad had not inherited storage facilities in Antonito, and if equipment failed to make the trip to Chama for safekeeping, it would suffer through the winter outside. Former Rio Grande Mikado No. 483, re-lettered for its new owner, was the first locomotive to operate on the restored railroad. By 1971, the Cumbres & Toltec was operating regular public excursions over its line.

Today the Cumbres & Toltec Scenic Railroad is jointly owned by Colorado and New Mexico and managed by the Cumbres & Toltec Scenic Railroad Commission. Trains are operated as a concession by a private company. During the railroad's nearly 30-year history, three different companies have handled operations. Restoration work is largely the result of the Friends of the Cumbres & Toltec, a volunteer organization committed to the preservation of the railroad, its structures, and equipment. The railroad is listed on the National Register of Historic Places and is subject to federal preservation regulations designed to help guide preservation efforts and maintain the railroad's authenticity.

Near the end of common carrier operations, a westbound freight train led by K-37 No. 493 pauses for water at Lava Tank on August 28, 1967. Mid-train helpers, as pictured here, were typically used on heavy westbound freights. John Gruber

On August 28, 1963, Rio Grande K-37 leads a train of Gramps oil tank cars. A second Mikado is cut in ahead of the caboose. John Gruber

Chapter 4

EAST BROAD TOP

T he Pennsylvania Central Railroad (later the Pennsylvania Railroad) built its standard gauge mainline along the Juniata River Valley in the 1850s, a major transportation improvement that facilitated industrial growth and settlement in this scenic rural region. Numerous branch lines were built in tributary valleys connecting outlying

The physical plant on the East Broad Top dates from another era. The stub switch seen here was an anachronism by the turn of the century—most switches use a system of movable points. East Broad Top's narrow gauge stub switches are among the last of their kind in North America.

Mikado No. 14 simmers in front of the roundhouse at Rockhill Furnace. It no longer pulls a train of empty hoppers up to the mines at Robertsdale—its days as a coal-hauling engine are long since past— but it still steams over the rails it was built for, and lives to see another day of service in the mountains of Pennsylvania.

Previous pages
A dense autumn fog prevails at East Broad Top's Rockhill Furnace shop complex. Mikado No. 15 eases off the turntable and is prepared for another day of work. The appearance of East Broad Top has changed very little in the last 50 years, and while this is autumn 1997, it could easily be 1947, or even 1927.

communities with the Pennsylvania mainline. One of these was the East Broad Top Railroad, built in the early 1870s south from a connection with the Pennsy at Mt. Union. It tapped into existing iron ore mines and helped develop coal fields on the east side of Broad Top Mountain. Iron ore had been mined since the mid-eighteenth century, and iron production was among the oldest established industries in the region. In addition to mines, smelting furnaces existed along Aughwick Creek, and many communities in the area, such as Rockhill Furnace, owe their names to their iron-producing heritage.

The EBT was one of the earliest American railways to select narrow gauge. Its management adopted 3-foot gauge in June 1872, about a year after the Rio Grande made the same choice.

The East Broad Top followed Aughwick Creek. Tracks reached Orbisonia, the location of Rockhill Furnace, 11 miles from Mt. Union, in August 1873. To tap the Broad Top coal fields, the railroad built farther south, passing through the villages of Three Springs and Saltillo, then

The sun fades beyond the mountains as No. 15 rolls northward through Rockhill Furnace past a set of disused coal hoppers. When East Broad Top bought a fleet of modern steel hoppers, it needed a stable of more powerful locomotives to haul them—thus it replaced its aging 2-8-0 Consolidations with new, modern Mikados from Baldwin.

began a steep, sinuous ascent into the mountains, climbing a 2.6 percent grade, piercing Sideling Hill with an 830-foot curved tunnel before dropping into Coles Valley. The line climbed a 2.7 percent grade and passed through a 1,235-foot tunnel beneath Wray's Hill. Beyond, the line followed Trough Creek and climbed toward Robertsdale (30 miles south of Mt. Union), the location of an important coal mine, which it reached in October 1874.

Several branches were built to reach other mines and additional traffic sources. East Broad Top began constructing an extension to reach the South Pennsylvania Railroad, a line being built by New York Central interests to compete with the Pennsylvania. However, the South Penn line was never completed (today it is the route of part of the Pennsylvania Turnpike, I-70), and the EBT extension only reached a mine near Shade Gap, although later extended a few more miles. In 1891, East Broad Top extended its mainline a few miles south to Woodvale, and ultimately to Alvan, 33 miles from Mt. Union. A few more branchline extensions were constructed, with the railroad achieving its maximum layout in 1916.

EBT located its offices, shops, roundhouse, and a yard at Rockhill Furnace near Orbisonia. A

East Broad Top No. 17 rolls through the shops at Rockhill Furnace on a clear October morning. Soon its tender will be topped off with coal and will be ready for a day of service. While East Broad Top survives as a colorful remnant of another era, it is representative of small town railroading that was once common throughout the United States.

sizable yard and coal-cleaning facility was built south of the PRR interchange at Mt. Union.

In its early years, the East Broad Top was integral to iron production in the region, by carrying iron ore and coal from local mines. A large portion of the coal carried by the railroad was consumed by online coke ovens for the production of iron products, which were then delivered

Mikado No 12, affectionately known as Millie is the smallest and oldest East Broad Top 2-8-2. It leads an afternoon double-header up a slight grade on the way to Orbisonia.

to the PRR at Mt. Union. A portion of Broad Top coal was transferred to the PRR for export to other regions, and EBT also carried ganister rock (used in brick manufacturing), timber, bricks, merchandise freight, and passenger traffic.

Decline of EBT

The railroad's iron traffic began to decline in the 1890s, dwindling away by World War I. Following the loss of iron traffic, East Broad Top experienced a great coal boom. Its high-water mark came in 1926, when about 80 percent of its freight traffic was coal. That year, according to narrow gauge authority George Hilton, the railroad moved greater than 25,725,000 ton miles. Shortly thereafter, coal mines along the EBT began to decline.

Highway traffic took business away from EBT and undermined the railroad's prosperity. During its peak, EBT operated two regularly scheduled passenger trains in each direction, but by the early 1930s, traffic was down to a single mixed train. Furthermore, timber shipments vanished, and the railroad lost most remaining merchandise traffic to the highway. In 1933, it simplified its interchange with the Pennsylvania Railroad by lifting standard gauge cars off their regular trucks and placing them on narrow gauge trucks.

Despite declining traffic and the worldwide economic depression of the 1930s—an event that left many railways insolvent nationwide—East Broad Top remained profitable through World War II. But to cut its losses and remain financially viable, the railway was forced to abandon several branches and scale back its operations.

East Broad Top No. 14 brings a train south from Colgate Grove. East Broad Top acquired most of its passenger equipment from the Boston, Revere Beach & Lynn, a narrow gauge commuter railroad in Massachusetts. Today, a remnant of the old BRB&L is operated by the Massachusetts Bay Transportation Authority as the Blue Line.

No. 17 leads a freight consist southbound toward Orbisonia on February 19, 1978. While the railroad ceased operation as a common carrier in 1956, it occasionally operates freight trains for the benefit of photographers. William R. Mischler, collection of Brian Jennison

Following the war, the railroad began to lose money: the coal market contracted rapidly in the late 1940s and early 1950s, and passenger service evaporated as the automobile began to dominate intercity transport. Mail trains were discontinued in 1953, and passenger service was discontinued the following year. Toward the end of its life, EBT's primary coal customers were brick plants in Mt. Union. But by 1955 coal, too, had declined, leaving only ganister stone as a major traffic source. That year the railroad applied to the Interstate Commerce Commission for abandonment, and in February 1956 it was granted. The railroad operated its last revenue train as a common carrier in mid-April 1956, and was then abandoned. In May 1956, the Kovalchick Salvage Company bought the line for scrap, including rolling stock and structures.

Preservation and Revival

Instead of scrapping the line, however, Nick Kovalchick recognized the nostalgic value of the East Broad Top line. In 1960, he began operating passenger excursions on a short portion of the line north of Orbisonia. Since that time, interest in the East Broad Top has grown. The National Park Service has investigated acquiring the property and developing it as an historical site. In 1990, the U.S. Government published a detailed report called Study of Alternatives for East Broad Top Railroad. However, as of this writing, the railroad, including shops, yards, locomotives, and cars, still remains the property of the Kovalchick

One of East Broad Top's greatest treasures is its turn-of-the-century shop facility complete with belt-driven machine tools. The railroad used these shops for the maintenance of its locomotives and freight car fleet. Mike Gardner

Self-propelled, gas-electric M-1 was delivered to EBT by the J.G. Brill company in kit form during 1926. It was assembled at the railroad's shops in 1927. Intended to help cut its passenger costs and operated in regular passenger service until 1953, M-1 is believed to have been the only true gas-electric built new for an American narrow gauge railway. Today it is the only remaining gas-electric in its original form.

family, who have faithfully operated the railroad as tourist carrier over the years.

About 3.5 miles of the line between the shops and yards at Rockhill Furnace and Colgate Grove is maintained for excursions. The remainder of the EBT lies derelict, but largely intact. Trees more than 40 feet tall grow between the rails. The tunnels at Sideling and Wray's Hills still have tracks through them, but these tracks have not seen service in more than 40 years. The offices, roundhouse, and shops at Orbisonia/ Rockhill Furnace remain as one of the best preserved examples of a turn-of-the-century railroad facility in North America.

Yet, despite great popular interest in the East Broad Top, its future is uncertain. Those wishing to experience this railway treasure should act soon, because whether it remains a private concern or eventually falls under the domain of a government agency, it is unlikely that the EBT will be as pure and uncluttered an experience as it is today. Although preserved from scrapping, it is not a museum, and with every passing year a little bit of the railroad fades.

Chapter 5

EVOLUTION OF NARROW GAUGE LOCOMOTIVES

The stationary steam engine was developed in Britain early in the eighteenth century as a pumping engine, and later adapted as a prime mover for industry. James Watt significantly improved the engine's

efficiency, and in 1781 introduced the double-acting reciprocating engine. He further improved the engine by converting reciprocating (back and forth) motion to rotary motion.

By 1800, there were more than a hundred steam engines working in mines and mills around Britain. At that time inventors in Britain, the United States, and France experimented with steam-powered conveyances and model steam locomotives. In 1803, a Cornishman, Richard Trevithick, constructed the first full-size steam locomotive for operation on the Pen-y-Darran Iron Works in Wales.

During the next 20 years, several talented men refined the steam locomotive for applications on industrial tram lines in collieries and mines in Britain. In 1821, the British Parliament authorized the Stockton & Darlington, the first steam railroad built for general transportation; it opened in 1825. The railway concept quickly spread in Britain and across the Atlantic to the United States.

The crew of Mikado No. 463 assumes a classic pose with their engine at Osier, Colorado, in June 1995. While the smallest of Rio Grande's 2-8-2 Mikado's, the K-27s were the largest, heaviest narrow gauge locomotives on the railroad when delivered in 1903. Known popularly as "Mud hens," the K-27s were the first Rio Grande locomotives built with outside frames and outside counterweights and crankpins. Brian Jennison

Previous pages
Rio Grande K-37 No. 497 leads Cumbres & Toltec train No. 2 up the west slope of Cumbres Pass. The K-37s are the heaviest and most powerful of the Rio Grande four Mikado classes. They produced a maximum 37,100 pounds tractive effort, 900 pounds more than the slightly lighter K-36s.

Sitting side by side at the Chama engine house are examples of Rio Grande's smallest and largest narrow gauge Mikados. On the left is K-27 "Mud hen" No. 463; on the right is K-37 No. 497. The K-37s were rebuilt from standard gauge 2-8-0 Consolidations by Rio Grande's Burnham shops in the late 1920s.

Most early American locomotives were based upon British designs and innovations, but were heavily adapted to the peculiarities of American railway operation. American locomotive builders tended to prefer locomotives with inside frames (between the wheels) and outside cylinders with outside rod connections, while British locomotive practice of that time favored outside frames and inside connected cylinders. American locomotives sported large pilots, known commonly as "cow-catchers." Furthermore, because of the less-refined nature of early American track structure, American locomotives needed greater flexibility than those operated in Britain. As a result, many locomotives built for road service (as opposed to switching service) employed a three-point suspension system using a set of leading wheels.

Baldwin Locomotive Works builder's plate for Denver & Rio Grande Western 2-8-2 Mikado, class K-36 No. 484, now in service on the Cumbres & Toltec Scenic Railroad. Baldwin was the prolific American steam locomotive builder and the largest supplier of narrow gauge locomotives.

A Rio Grande class K-36 displays its distinctive running gear in the afternoon sun at Chama, New Mexico. Rio Grande's narrow gauge Mikados employed outside frames, outside crankpins and counterweights, instead of the conventional arrangement normally used on standard gauge locomotives. This arrangement permitted the construction of a significantly larger, more powerful narrow gauge locomotive.

Some narrow gauge lines used 0-4-4T Forney tank locomotives (hence the T in 0-4-4T), which incorporated water and coal storage on the locomotive without the use of a separate tender. The weight of water and coal was centered on the rear trailing truck to avoid changes in tractive effort as the locomotive exhausted its fuel. This Forney was built for Maine's 2-foot gauge Monson Railroad. In later years it served Edaville in South Carver, Mass. William R. Mischler, collection of Brian Jennison

Steam locomotives are classified and identified by wheel arrangement using the Whyte system: the first number indicates the number of leading wheels, the middle number (or numbers) indicates driving wheels, and the last represents trailing wheels. A zero would indicate a lack of wheels in that section of locomotive. Thus a 2-8-0 type would have two leading wheels, eight driving wheels, and no trailing wheels. Locomotive types are usually given a distinctive name and may be referred to by wheel arrangement, name, or both.

By the 1870s, the dominant wheel arrangements used by standard gauge locomotives in the United States were the 4-4-0 "American," 4-6-0 "Ten Wheeler," 2-6-0 "Mogul," and 2-8-0 "Consolidation."

Typical Nineteenth Century Narrow Gauge Locomotives

Narrow gauge railways, unheard of in the United States prior to 1870, became one of the fastest-growing segments of the railroad industry during the 1870s and early 1880s. More than 20 different builders constructed narrow gauge locomotives, and between 1870 and 1890 more than 1,400 3-foot gauge engines were built in the United States for common carrier service (as opposed to industrial use). Baldwin, the predominant locomotive builder in the United States, claimed the largest share of the narrow gauge locomotive market, building 561 narrow gauge locomotives for American common carriers in that period.

The vast majority of 3-foot gauge locomotives built in the United States for common carrier railroads before the turn of the century were simply smaller versions of standard gauge locomotive types. These early narrow gauge engines did not employ any specialized equipment and did not represent a significant evolution in locomotive development. They used conventional boilers, cylinders, and valve gear. For the most part, they used wheel arrangements popular on standard gauge locomotives. The most popular type in numbers sold was the 2-6-0 Mogul: roughly 450 were built to 3-foot gauge specifications. The Mogul was followed by the 4-4-0 American and 2-8-0 Consolidation in popularity.

Narrow gauge railroad building in the United States peaked in 1883 and then rapidly waned. By the mid-1880s, hundreds of miles of narrow gauge were being converted to standard gauge, and there was very little new narrow gauge railway construction. As a result, the locomotives purchased during the first dozen years of the narrow gauge boom were more than sufficient to handle narrow gauge railroad traffic, and few lines had a need to acquire more new power. Comparatively few narrow gauge steam locomotives were built after 1883, and despite many advances in locomotive technology, few innovations were implemented to domestic narrow gauge locomotives until after the turn of the century.

During the 1890s, the trend in standard gauge American steam locomotive development was toward larger, more powerful freight locomotives, and faster, more powerful passenger locomotives. Locomotive builders introduced a variety of design improvements intended to produce greater power and speed, and to improve fuel efficiency. One popular innovation was the compound locomotive, which reused steam to achieve greater efficiency by employing a system of both high- and low-pressure cylinders. The addition of a rear swiveling truck allowed for a substantially larger firebox, and thereby a much more powerful locomotive. Since lightly built narrow gauge lines were not well suited for either fast or exceptionally powerful locomotives, there was little need to incorporate such improvements on new narrow gauge locomotives.

By the turn of the twentieth century, most narrow gauge locomotives were technological antiques. Narrow gauge expert George Hilton points out that some narrow gauge railways never had the need to acquire new locomotives and

In 1923 Alco built 10 class K-28 Mikados for Rio Grande. Known popularly as "Sport Models" these locomotives were regularly assigned to passenger trains. Durango & Silverton No. 478 leads an excursion at Silverton, Colorado. The D&S has three serviceable K-28s.

operated throughout their existence with their original locomotives.

The Rio Grande and East Broad Top were unusual American narrow gauge lines, modernizing their narrow gauge motive power fleets after the turn of the century.

Early Motive Power on the Denver & Rio Grande

With great celebration, William Jackson Palmer's Denver & Rio Grande operated its first train from Denver to Colorado Springs behind a diminutive Baldwin 2-4-0, named *Montezuma*, which weighed only 25,000 pounds. During its first years, the D&RG operated with just twelve Baldwin locomotives: four 2-4-0s, including the *Montezuma*, for passenger service, and eight 2-6-0s for freight service. The 2-4-0 was relatively rare in America, but the 2-6-0 Mogul was the predominant nineteenth century narrow gauge freight hauler, serving D&RG well during its first half-dozen years.

As the line grew, however, traffic increased, and D&RG needed more powerful locomotives. The industry responded, making later 2-6-0s significantly larger and more powerful than early models. The first batch of 2-6-0s weighed 35,000 pounds and produced 4,750 pounds of tractive effort, while later 2-6-0s, built in 1876, weighed 46,000 pounds and produced 7,060 pounds of tractive effort.

A letter dated February 13, 1877, from D&RG's W. W. Borst to Burnham, Parry Williams & Company (originally printed in a 1877 Baldwin narrow gauge locomotive catalog titled *Narrow Gauge Locomotives*, and reprinted by the University of Oklahoma Press in 1967 with a foreword by Laurence S. Reid), details the daily work of D&RG's later 2-6-0s: "The average train for these engines is twelve loaded box or thirteen loaded coal cars and caboose . . . 150 tons of cars and lading." Borst continues, "Our average freight train time [recorded] is 10 miles per hour between Denver and Pueblo. On heavy grades speed is reduced to 8 miles, and on slightly descending grades [and level track] the speed is increased to 12 miles."

Denver & Rio Grande's heavily graded mountain lines, especially those built after 1875, taxed the abilities of even its largest 2-6-0s. As its traffic grew, the railroad sought a more powerful locomotive that could provide greater tractive effort but would not require a substantial upgrading of tracks and bridges—a fairly typical objective for a railroad of the time.

Rio Grande's Fairlie

Palmer's association with British narrow gauge promoter and locomotive designer Robert Fairlie led him to order one of Fairlie's double-ended locomotives, similar to those used on the Festiniog line in Wales. Fairlie specifically

Rio Grande's K-28s were its only narrow gauge 2-8-2 Mikados built by Alco; all the others were Baldwin products. During World War II, seven K-28s were sent to the White Pass & Yukon in Alaska where they served for a short time. After the war they were scrapped. The three remaining K-28s now operate on the Durango & Silverton. Number 478 waits at Durango in August of 1991.

Durango & Silverton K-36 No. 481 leads a returning excursion toward Durango in September 1998. Each of the four classes of Rio Grande Mikados occupies a distinct number sequence. The K-27s were numbered in the 450s and 460s, K-28s as 470s, K-36s as 480s, and K-37s as 490s.

designed his locomotives for narrow gauge service with the intention of producing an engine with pulling power comparable to that of a standard gauge locomotive.

Denver & Rio Grande's Fairlie was built by the Vulcan Foundry Company in England, and delivered to the railroad in June 1873. Like most later double-ended Fairlies, it featured twin fireboxes to avoid draft problems that had plagued Fairlie's first machine. Each firebox had a grate area of 12 square feet. This unique locomotive was 28 feet long, had four 10x18 inch cylinders and two pairs of 39 inch driving wheels, each mounted on a swiveling bogie. It weighed 62,000 pounds and produced an estimated 9,280 pounds tractive effort.

Appropriately named *Mountaineer*, the double-ended locomotive was mostly assigned to helper service on D&RG's rugged La Veta Pass (or Veta Pass) crossing. It served the D&RG for about 10 years, and was scrapped about 1888. It was the only narrow gauge Fairlie type built for service in the United States, and was not viewed favorably by operating men or the railroad. Hilton states that the locomotive cost approximately three times as much as early Baldwin 2-6-0s, and while it could haul about a third more tonnage, it was less efficient to operate.

Narrow gauge lines in other parts of the world had considerably better luck with the Fairlie design. The Festiniog Railway successfully employed Fairlies in revenue service for more than 70 years, and lines in Canada, Mexico, and South America also had success with the Fairlies. It is not known why the Fairlie fared so poorly in

Cumbres & Toltec K-36 No. 487 waits at Chama, New Mexico, in September 1996. This locomotive sports a large plow designed for combating heavy snow in the mountains. The plow is removable and does not identify the locomotive. Beneath the plow is a more typical pilot, often described as a "cow-catcher."

Colorado, but the *Mountaineer* remains a singular unsuccessful curiosity on the Denver & Rio Grande. Had the locomotive performed better for D&RG, the Fairlie type may have become more common on American narrow gauge lines.

William Mason, an innovative New England builder, modified Fairlie's concept and built single-truck swiveling locomotives, commonly referred to as "Mason Bogie" engines. In order to cope with space problems relating to the swiveling bogie, Mason adopted Walschaert's outside valve gear. (Valve gear is integral to the operation of a steam locomotive, allowing the locomotive engineer to set the valves and thus control the power and direction of the engine.) Mason is credited for the first American adaptation of this popular outside valve gear, which became widespread in America after 1900.

Mason was much more successful than Fairlie in marketing narrow gauge locomotives in America, yet Mason's locomotives remained relatively obscure. There were nearly 90 Mason Bogies built for narrow gauge lines. A large number were used by the Boston, Revere Beach & Lynn, a suburban passenger line that operated northeast of Boston, Massachusetts. Rio Grande's neighbor and competitor, Denver, South Park & Pacific, also successfully employed a fleet of Mason Bogies; it was the only Colorado railroad to use them.

More Practical Mountain Power

In the 1870s, the 2-8-0 Consolidation was becoming the standard freight locomotive type in the United States. The wheel arrangement was so named because among its first users was the Lehigh Valley Railroad, a Pennsylvania line that had just merged or "consolidated" with the Lehigh & Mahanoy Railroad, whose master mechanic had just adopted the type for mountain service. Its four pairs of driving wheels provided excellent tractive effort and spread out the locomotive weight for less stress to light track and bridges.

On a glorious, clear New Mexico morning, Baldwin-built K-36 No. 488 is readied for its trip over Cumbres Pass to Antonito, Colorado. The 10 K-36s were the last narrow gauge locomotives built new for Rio Grande. The slightly larger K-37s were built later, but were not considered "new" because they were rebuilt from old standard gauge engines.

Rio Grande 2-8-0 Consolidation No. 268 leads a freight near Crested Butte, Colorado, on October 3, 1953. Rio Grande relied upon 2-8-0s for the majority of its narrow gauge freight service during the last two decades of the nineteenth century. In most respects these Consolidations were simply smaller versions of those used on standard gauge lines. Otto C. Perry, Denver Public Library, Western History Department

In 1908, veteran railroad photographer Fred Jukes photographed a pair of D&RG 2-8-0 Consolidations with an eastbound freight at Chama, New Mexico. Consolidations remained as standard mainline locomotives on the San Juan Extension longer than elsewhere on Rio Grande's 3-foot gauge network, because the track could not accommodate the newer, heavier Mikados that are now associated with operations on the Cumbres & Toltec. Fred Jukes, Denver Public Library Western History Department

Robert Fairlie intended his double-ended locomotive to rival the pulling power of a comparable standard gauge engine. Although popular elsewhere, Palmer's Rio Grande acquired just one Fairlie type, named Mountaineer, seen on La Veta Pass where it was assigned as a helper. It is distinguished from its Welsh counterparts by typically American accouterments: diamond smoke stacks, wooden "cowcatcher" and large headlight. Denver Public Library Western History Department

Early Baldwin narrow gauge Consolidations would place between 11,000 and 12,500 pounds on each driving axle, weight per axle comparable to that of Mogul types. If new locomotives had a much greater weight per axle than existing locomotives, substantial upgrading of bridges and track structure might be required before the weighty locomotives could operate safely. Baldwin advertised the Consolidation as being "especially adapted to heavy freight service." To better negotiate sharp curves, and put less wear on track, only two of the four pairs of driving wheels were flanged.

In 1877 Denver & Rio Grande bought its first 2-8-0 Consolidation. The wheel arrangement proved well suited to the D&RG's mountain lines, and the type was adopted as D&RG's standard freight power, remaining so for roughly a quarter-century. Ultimately, the line owned more than 150 3-foot gauge 2-8-0s, nearly half of all narrow gauge 2-8-0s built in the United States for common carrier service. They were used all over D&RG's vast narrow gauge system, from the mainlines over the Palmer Divide and Marshall Pass, to the Leadville and San Juan mining districts.

Twentieth Century Power

High in the Rockies, near the New Mexico—Colorado line, a diminutive, aged Mikado pours forth black coal smoke from its stack as it struggles up the grueling 4 percent grade toward Cumbres Pass. Compared to most modern steam locomotives, this machine, Rio Grande K27 No. 463, seems small, compact, and archaic. In fact, the K27 is the smallest and oldest class of Rio Grande's Mikados.

Throughout the nineteenth century, firebox size was a principal limiting factor of locomotive power potential. The traditional firebox placement between locomotive frames greatly restricted its size. Many early attempts at building large locomotives failed because of inadequate firebox capacity, which would result in insufficient steam to sustain the engine under load. Narrow gauge locomotives, because of their smaller size, faced significantly greater firebox restrictions than their standard gauge counterparts.

The introduction of the weight-bearing rear-swiveling truck permitted the firebox to sit above the frames and behind the driving wheels, allowing for a dramatic increase in size. The firebox-bearing rear-swiveling truck was applied to American freight locomotives after the turn of the century with the domestic introduction of the 2-8-2 Mikado type, a logical enlargement of the successful 2-8-0 Consolidation.

The 2-8-2 was developed by Baldwin in the 1890s as an export locomotive. It got its colorful moniker because Japan was one of the first large buyers of the type at a time when Gilbert & Sullivan's opera about the Japanese Emperor, *The Mikado,* was enjoying great popularity in the United States.

Mud Hens

The adaptation of the Mikado to narrow gauge proportions was very important to Denver & Rio Grande, which was among the earliest domestic railways to use it. D&RG acquired 15 3-foot gauge

While Rio Grande was the first and most widespread narrow gauge railroad in Colorado, it was not the only one. Second to Rio Grande in length was the Denver, South Park & Pacific. The DSP&P operated a small fleet of Mason Bogie engines, a single truck adaptation of the Fairlie type that enjoyed limited popularity in the United States. This rare photograph shows a DSP&P Mason Bogie at Nathrop Station near Alpine Pass. Collier, Denver Public Library Western History Department

K27 2-8-2 Mikados from Baldwin in 1903. The K27 combined several evolutionary developments, making it significantly different from most locomotives used by American narrow gauge lines.

The K27 employed outside frames—most American locomotives had inside frames—and used outside counterweights and crankpins. (The K27 was not the first outside-frame narrow gauge locomotive—Baldwin designed and built some outside-frame narrow gauge locomotives in the 1880s for export purposes, but the sagging economy of narrow gauge railroading precluded any American lines from taking advantage of this innovation at the time. Baldwin also built several outside-frame Consolidations for Colorado's Crystal River Railroad in 1900.) The K27s were built as Vauclain compounds, Baldwin's preferred method of reusing steam, featuring two sets of high- and low-pressure cylinders. These were the only narrow gauge compounds built for the Rio Grande.

Later, compound locomotives fell out of favor, largely because the costs of maintaining

Rio Grande employed a large fleet of 2-8-0 Consolidations to haul its freight. Today Rio Grande No. 346 resides at the Colorado Railroad Museum in Golden. It was built by Baldwin in 1881 and is one of the oldest serviceable steam locomotives in America.

the more complex equipment exceeded cost savings achieved through greater efficiency. So, consistent with the national trend, D&RG's K27s were rebuilt into simple locomotives with 17x23 inch cylinders. As simple engines, they produced roughly 27,000 pounds tractive effort.

When the K27s were introduced, they were known to railroad men as "Monsters" because they were vastly larger than anything else ever seen on the narrow gauge. They were designed to haul a 220-ton train up D&RG's steep mountain grades, making them twice as powerful as the railroad's older Consolidations. But the K27s were too large to work on most of the narrow gauge system. For their first few years, they were restricted to service between Salida and Sargent on the former narrow gauge mainline over Marshall Pass. Before World War I, the D&RG upgraded the west slope of Cumbres Pass with heavier rail specifically to allow its "Monsters" to operate as helper locomotives between Chama and the summit. When new, the K27s were state-of-the-art machines, vastly superior technologically to the 25-year-old relics that composed the majority of D&RG's narrow gauge locomotive fleet.

Today, Rio Grande's K27s are known affectionately as "Mud Hens"—a name that seems to have originated either because in their earliest days the big engines often derailed, landing in the dirt, or perhaps because they stirred up the dirt ballast in the fashion of a bathing barnyard chicken.

K28s

After buying its K27s, two decades passed before Rio Grande ordered additional new narrow gauge locomotives—although in 1916 it acquired outside-frame Consolidations from the Crystal River Railroad. When Rio Grande finally placed its order it chose the outside-frame Mikado, but this time from Baldwin's competitor, Alco. By 1923, new narrow gauge steam locomotives were a curiosity, and Hilton notes that only

12 3-foot gauge engines were built new for domestic common carrier use that year; 10 of those were D&RG's Alco-built class K28s.

The K28 was slightly larger than the K27 and slightly more powerful, providing roughly 27,540 pounds tractive effort with 44-inch drivers. It was capable of maintaining a steady 40 miles per hour and quickly became the preferred narrow gauge passenger locomotive.

Last of the Mikados

In 1925, the Rio Grande ordered an additional 10 outside-frame Mikados from Baldwin, denoted class K36. These were the last narrow gauge locomotives built new for the railroad, and were substantially heavier and more powerful than the K27s and K28s. They weighed 187,000 pounds and developed 36,200 pounds tractive effort, a third more than the older Mikados. The K36s are the most common type used on the Cumbres & Toltec today.

The final narrow gauge locomotives to enter service on the Rio Grande were 10 K37 outside-frame Mikados rebuilt from turn-of-the-century standard gauge Consolidations by the company's Burnham shops between 1928 and 1930. These were Rio Grande's most powerful narrow gauge steam locomotives.

East Broad Top Locomotives

In its early years, East Broad Top operated a fleet of 2-6-0 Moguls and 2-8-0 Consolidations, traditional narrow gauge locomotive types found on many lines. In 1908, the railroad purchased a single 2-6-2 Prairie type. By 1911 the East Broad Top had evolved into primarily a coal hauler. The railroad was an unusually progressive narrow gauge operator, and sought to upgrade its locomotive and rolling stock fleet with new, modern equipment. The upgrade was a significant investment, and unusual because, except for the Rio Grande, few other narrow gauge lines had even considered new locomotives or rolling stock. East Broad Top took delivery of a new steel hopper car fleet in 1913. Between 1911 and 1920, the railroad purchased six new 2-8-2 Mikados from Baldwin. The first, No. 12, was the smallest of the new engines. However, like Rio Grande's K27 Mud hens, No. 12 was by far the largest, most powerful locomotive on the railroad when it was delivered.

To accommodate larger, heavier locomotives, the EBT rebuilt its track with heavier rail and strengthened its bridges. Mikados Nos. 14 and 15 were 17 tons heavier than No. 12 and slightly more powerful, but the last three locomotives were the largest, Nos. 16, 17, and 18, which weighed 81 tons each.

These big locomotives came equipped with modern equipment, including superheaters and piston valves (as opposed to older "D" type slide

East Broad Top No. 17 at the Rockhill Furnace shops in October 1997. Presently four of East Broad Top's six narrow gauge 2-8-2s are serviceable. Number 17 is one of the larger Mikados and is usually operated only a couple times a year. It's one of the only operable locomotives left in the United States that uses Southern valve gear. The last three East Broad Top Mikados were delivered with this type of valve gear instead of the far more typical Walschaerts.

East Broad Top, like Rio Grande, took the atypical step of modernizing its narrow gauge locomotive fleet during the early part of the twentieth century, purchasing six Baldwin-built Mikados between 1911 and 1920. These locomotives do not use outside frames and counterweights like Rio Grande's Mikados, instead employing a more conventional arrangement. East Broad Top No. 15 leads an excursion southbound toward Orbisonia, Pennsylvania.

Detailed view of the Southern valve gear on East Broad Top No. 17. Valve gear is an integral part of the locomotive that allows the engineer to control the valves in order to regulate the power and direction of the locomotive. Southern derives its motion entirely from an eccentric connected to drivers and does not involve a crosshead connection as does Walschaerts gear.

Detailed view of the Walschaerts valve gear on East Broad Top No. 15. This was a typical outside valve gear arrangement used on twentieth century steam locomotives. Walschaerts uses both an eccentric attached to the running gear and a crosshead connection to obtain valve motion.

valves), and used Southern Valve gear, rather than Walschaerts. While superheaters and piston valves had become standard equipment on most new locomotives, Southern Valve gear was highly unusual, and these three East Broad Top locomotives are believed to be some of the only narrow gauge engines to use this variety of outside-valve gear. The three big Mikados were capable of hauling 22 loaded steel coal-hoppers, carrying roughly 700 tons of coal, up the ruling northbound grade from the mines to Mt. Union.

In addition to its narrow gauge fleet, EBT also operated two standard gauge Baldwin 0-6-0 switchers at its Mt. Union interchange with the Pennsylvania Railroad.

Today all six East Broad Top Mikados remain on the property. While Nos. 16 and 18 have not run in more than 40 years, the other four locomotives are serviceable. When they are not hauling excursions, these old engines reside where they always have, in the solid stone roundhouse at Rock Hill Furnace. Usually either No. 14 or 15 is called for regular excursion service, while 12 and 17 are reserved for special occasions.

During its annual Fall Spectacular, the railroad normally fires up all four serviceable Mikes and puts on a splendid show. Where else east of the Rocky Mountains can you find four steaming Mikados? The astute observer will readily distinguish each of the four by sound alone. Each engine has its own distinctive whistle: old No. 12 has a low mournful wail, while No. 17's whistle is a high-pitched shriek. Mikados No. 14 and No. 15 fall in between. When No. 12 whistles up the valley, calling out over the hills and trees as it has done for nearly a century, it is a romantic and fleeting sound from another era.

BIBLIOGRAPHY

Books

Athearn, Robert G. *Rebel of the Rockies: The Denver & Rio Grande Western Railroad.* New Haven, CT, 1962.

Beebe, Lucius and Charles Clegg. *Narrow Gauge in the Rockies.* Berkeley, CA, 1958.

Best, Gerald M. *Snowplow: Clearing Mountain Rails.* Berkeley, CA, 1966.

Boyd, J. I. C. *The Festiniog Railway, Vols. 1 & 2.* England, 1975.

Bruce, Alfred W. *The Steam Locomotive in America.* New York, NY, 1952.

Conrad, J. David. *The Steam Locomotive Directory of North America, Volumes 1 & 2.* Polo, IL, 1988.

Crump, Spencer. *Riding the Cumbres & Toltec Scenic Railroad.* Corona del Mar, CA, 1992.

Drury, George H. *Guide to North American Steam Locomotives.* Waukesha, WI, 1993.

Dunscomb, Guy L. *A Century of Southern Pacific Steam Locomotives.* Modesto, CA, 1963.

Ferrell, Mallory Hope. *Colorful East Broad Top.* Forest Park, IL, 1993.

Forney, M. N. *Catechism of the Locomotive.* New York, NY, 1876.

Grenard, Ross, and Frederick A. Kramer. *East Broad Top to the Mines and Back.* Newton, NJ, 1990.

Hauck, Cornelius W. *Colorado Rail Annual No. 10: Narrow Gauge to Silver Plume.* Golden, CO, 1972.

Hendry, R. Powell. *Narrow Gauge Story.* Rugby, England, 1979.

Hilton, George W. *American Narrow Gauge Railroads.* Stanford, CA, 1990.

LeMassena, Robert A. *Colorado's Mountain Railroads.* Golden, CO, 1963.

LeMassena, Robert A. *Rio Grande to the Pacific.* Denver, CO, 1974.

McCoy, Dell, and Russ Collman. *The Crystal River Pictorial.* Denver, CO, 1972.

McCoy, Dell, and Russ Collman. *"The Rio Grande Pictorial": One Hundred Years of Railroading thru the Rockies.* Denver, CO, 1971.

Mellander, Deane E. *East Broad Top—Slim Gauge Survivor.* Silver Spring, MD, 1995.

Osterwald, Doris B. *Cinders & Smoke.* Lakewood, CO, 1995.

Osterwald, Doris B. *Ticket to Toltec.* Denver, CO, 1992.

Quiett, Glenn Chesney. *They Built the West.* New York, NY, 1934.

Ransome, P. T. J. *Narrow Gauge Steam.* Oxford, 1996.

Ransome-Wallis, P. *World Railway Locomotives.* New York, NY, 1959.

Reid, Laurance S. *Narrow Gauge Locomotives: The Baldwin Catalog of 1877.* Norman, OK, 1967.

Sinclair, Angus. *Development of the Locomotive Engine.* New York, NY, 1907.

Solomon, Brian. *American Steam Locomotive.* Osceola, WI, 1998.

Swengel, Frank M. *The American Steam Locomotive: Volume 1, Evolution.* Davenport, IA, 1967.

White, John H., Jr. *Early American Locomotives.* Toronto, 1972.

Wilson, O. Meredith. *The Denver and Rio Grande Project, 1870—1901.* Salt Lake City, UT, 1982.

Winther, Oscar Osburn. *The Transportation Frontier: Trans-Mississippi West, 1865—1890.* New York, NY, 1964.

Ziel, Ron. *American Locomotives in Historic Photographs.* New York, NY, 1993.

Periodicals

Locomotive & Railway Preservation. Waukesha, WI (no longer published)

RailNews. Waukesha, WI

Railroad History, formerly *Railway and Locomotive Historical Society Bulletin.* Boston, MA

Trains. Waukesha, WI

Vintage Rails. Waukesha, WI

INDEX